REGENTS CRITICS SERIES

General Editor: Paul A. Olson

SIR PHILIP SIDNEY'S
DEFENSE OF POESY

Other volumes in the Regents Critics Series are:

Sir Philip Sidney's Defense of Poesy

Edited by

LEWIS SOENS

UNIVERSITY OF NEBRASKA PRESS · LINCOLN

Publishers on the Plains

UNP

Copyright © 1970 by the University of Nebraska Press
International Standard Book Number 0–8032–0464–7
Library of Congress Catalog card number 74–108900

For Mark Stevens and Tom Kassler

MANUFACTURED IN THE UNITED STATES OF AMERICA

Regents Critics Series

The Regents Critics Series provides reading texts of significant literary critics in the Western tradition. The series treats criticism as a useful tool: an introduction to the critic's own poetry and prose if he is a poet or novelist, an introduction to other work in his day if he is more judge than creator. Nowhere is criticism regarded as an end in itself but as what it is—a means to the understanding of the language of art as it has existed and been understood in various periods and societies.

Each volume includes a scholarly introduction which describes how the work collected came to be written, and suggests its uses. All texts are edited in the most conservative fashion consonant with the production of a good reading text; and all translated texts observe the dictum that the letter gives life and the spirit kills when a technical or rigorous passage is being put into English. Other types of passages may be more freely treated. Footnoting and other scholarly paraphernalia are restricted to the essential minimum. Such features as a bibliographical checklist or an index are carried where they are appropriate to the work in hand. If a volume is the first collection of the author's critical writing, this is noted in the bibliographical data.

PAUL A. OLSON

University of Nebraska

Contents

Introduction

Sir Philip Sidney's *Defense of Poesy* reflects the Renaissance Idea of what literary criticism ought to be, just as Sidney himself embodied the Idea of what a courtier should be. Sidney synthesized the work of the great fifteenth- and sixteenth-century Italian and French critics from Petrarch to Du Bellay (including such men as Minturno, Scaliger, Robortellus, and Castelvetro). He may also have been as seminal to the new poetic growth of the late sixteenth and early seventeenth centuries as Ezra Pound was to the growth of early twentieth-century poetry, for the distinguished poetry which lights the 1580s, '90s, and later, particularly in the *Faery Queen* and in *Paradise Lost*, probably would not have blazed quite as high as it did without the critical achievement of Sidney's *Defense*.[1] Sidney was able to have such an effect because he disciplined an aesthetic rooted in traditional Christian humanism (a humanism which had appropriated the pagan gold found in Plato, Cicero, Virgil, and a recently re-discovered Aristotle) to the service of a Protestant and increasingly Puritan culture. He provided an instrument, in his poetic theory, which may have helped Protestant humanists such as Spenser and Milton to soften the craggy features of their Puritanism. As a philosophic critic, Sidney fused the ontological exaltation of the Neo-Platonists, the analytic subtlety of the Aristotelians, and the practical sagacity of the Ciceronian and Horatian rhetorics. He thus forged an implement fit to the hands of poets who wished to help in

---

1. See J. E. Spingarn, *Literary Criticism in the Renaissance*, 2nd ed. (New York: Harbinger, 1963), p. 170; A. C. Hamilton, *The Structure of Allegory in the Faery Queen* (Oxford: Oxford University Press, 1961), pp. 56, 125; C. S. Lewis, *English Literature in the Sixteenth Century* (Oxford: Oxford University Press, 1954), p. 343; John Buxton, *Sir Philip Sidney and the English Renaissance* (New York: St. Martin's 1965), p. 255. W. R. Davis, *Idea and Act in Elizabethan Fiction* (Princeton: Princeton University Press, 1969), p. 28, credits Sidney with writing the only Elizabethan critical treatise that "squarely faces the problem of imaginative fiction."

the Protestant, perhaps Calvinist, task of regenerating men to fit them to live in a godly Christian commonwealth.

Sidney's implement was valuable. Increasingly those Protestants and Puritans who wished to make men better and to keep them so through poetry had yielded to the Calvinist and extremist argument that only the Bible could do this. Sidney's *Defense* argued that secular poetry did not claim to do the same work as the Bible, but that it accomplished a task which supplemented that book's divine poetry. Sidney thus gave to secular poetry a Protestant and Neo-Platonist justification. The value of his work does not lie in any single phrase or idea, but rather in the coherence and unity of moral end which he gave to Renaissance commonplaces of criticism, and the sober delight which he infused into this coherence. Sidney welded the commonplaces which he used into a whole by arguing that the poet is a man who see the "Ideas" of the virtues as they may be conceived to exist in Plato's ideal world (which is also the "golden world" of Greek and Roman myth and Adam's pre-lapsarian world, Eden). The poet sees these things because he has a divinely endowed natural reason, a mind whose eyes God has cleared. His vision of the Idea-world, the noumenal world, so fills him with admiration and delight that it impels him to seek to develop the rhetorical skill which will enable him to let his audience share in his experience. This they can do insofar as his rhetorical skill gives to the Ideas a local habitation and a name apprehensible from the perspective of the audience's experience of this world. Thus the poet permits his readers to experience iconically something analogous to his own poetic and special experience of the ideal world. He clears their eyes to see, know, and love that world. When Sidney says that the poet creates a golden world for his reader, he means nothing less than that the experience of poetry is an experience of Adam's uncorrupted, prelapsarian virtue and a conversation with the "Ideas," or *eidola*, of human natural perfection as easy as Adam's with the angels.

In developing this argument, Sidney displays the critical syncretism of the Renaissance. He draws felicitously from commonplaces associated with Cicero and the rhetoricians, with Aristotle and his commentators and imitators, with Plato and the platonizing critics of the French and Italian academies. He also draws on commentators on the Bible and writers of biblically inspired poetry. His special service is to combine these commonplaces in a way designed to give the poet who wrote in Elizabeth's England and in the Queen's English the sense that his poetry *could* help fit men to live in the commonwealth of good men, and to give the reader who belonged to the same England the sense of how *English* poetry could do this.

Poetry needed the sort of defense Sidney developed. It was under attack for corrupting men. The Puritan Stephen Gosson in his *School of Abuse* (1579) (which may have precipitated Sidney's *Defense*)[2] doubted that secular poetry could reform men and argued that, in practice, poetry usually further corrupts the already corrupted. Other people close to Sidney argued in a similar vein. Sidney was the brilliant and poetical nephew of the Earl of Leicester, and many members of Leicester's intellectual entourage were skeptical of the possible value of secular or pagan poetry as compared to that of history and other utilitarian literature: for example, Thomas Blundeville, in his *True Order and Method of Writing and Reading Histories* (1574), attacked secular poetry and exalted history as the supreme moral art because it could supply instances of Providence in action and examples of good to be sought and evil to be eschewed.[3] (Other members of the Leicester circle were more liberal.) Similar attacks on poetry were being made on the Continent. Sidney, however, was not quarreling with Gosson, or anyone else, in any urgent and basic way. His chase had a larger beast in view: the general justification, against narrow attack, of art not explicitly Christian in content.

Sidney indicates the direction which his defense will take when, after defining poetry, he divides it into three classes, and specifies

2. See William A. Ringler, Jr., *Stephen Gosson* (Princeton: Princeton University Press, 1942), pp. 117–122, for a discussion of the parallels between the *Defense* and Gosson's *School*.

3. See Eleanor Rosenberg, *Leicester, Patron of Letters* (New York: Columbia University Press, 1955), pp. 14–15, 182–183. Lily B. Campbell, *Divine Poetry and Drama in Sixteenth Century England* (Berkeley: University of California Press, 1959), pp. 3–4, says that both Catholics and Protestants turned to divine poetry to combat a rising taste for pagan classics. See also G. G. Smith, ed., *Elizabethan Critical Essays* (Oxford: Clarendon Press, 1904), I, xiv–xxi.

that class which he wishes to defend. The three classes are: (1) religious or "Divine" poetry, that is the directly inspired religious poetry of the Bible (or poetry explicitly based on the Bible) and classical hymnic or orphic poetry; (2) philosophic poetry, that is versified discursive writing of a learned sort (Cato, Lucretius, Lucan); and (3) "right poetry," that is, the "feigning" of things as they "may be" or "ought to be." This "right poetry," made up of meaningful fictions, is the poetry Sidney intends to defend.

Sidney's choice of what he wished to defend was quite deliberate. He knew that he did not have to defend the first kind of poetry since the most narrowly fundamentalist Protestant would scarcely attack the "Divine poetry" of the Bible, inspired as it was directly by the Holy Ghost.[4] The fundamentalist might quarrel with the theology implicit in the orphic hymns, but they were hardly a major issue in the Renaissance. Sidney did not have to defend the second kind of poetry, philosophic poetry; he knew that Lucan and Lucretius might or might not qualify as poets, depending upon a grammarian's definition which might specify either that the distinguishing feature of poetry is that it is written in verse, or that the feature is that it expresses itself through "feigning," i.e., fiction. If the second definition is accepted, philosophic "poetry" is removed from the realm by definition. But the third kind of poetry, "right poetry," did not spring explicitly from the Bible or from immediate divine inspiration, and it did not speak learned truth discursively. It had roots in the pagan genres—the heroic, the comic, the satiric, and so forth; its differentiating feature was fiction, not verse; it used Plato's "lies." But to Sidney, right poetry, far from lying, embodies the truths of that most austere and hackneyed of subjects, morality.[5]

4. Anthony Gilbie remarks that the Psalms are "a briefe & a plaine declaration of the meaning of the holy Ghost, who did endite the Psalmes, and set them foorth by his secretaries, David and others, as shall appeare within their places" (Gilbie, trans., *The Psalmes of David Truely Opened and Explained* [1580], by Theodore Beza, fol. ¶ 2ᵛ.

5. The defense of pagan poetry as a moral transmutation of "Egyptian gold" was a fairly popular occupation in the Renaissance. See P. A. Olson, "A note on John Bromyard and Augustine's *Christian Doctrine*," *English Language Notes* (1966), pp. 165–168, for a discussion of the use of the phrase "Egyptian gold" for pagan poetry in popular symbology. Frances A. Yates, *The French Academies*

Its purpose is to make the good experienced and loved:[6]

> [Poets] indeed do merely make to imitate, and imitate both to delight
> and teach, and delight to move men to take that goodness in hand
> which, without delight, they would fly as from a stranger, and teach to
> make them know that goodness whereunto they are moved . . . .[7]

To forward the general justification of such poetry, poetry overtly
non-religious in subject matter, Sidney argues that the poet's
fictions contribute to an end which the Protestant sought in his
daily work and prayer, whether in Geneva, England, or, later, New
England: the regenerate man living in a godly commonwealth in
this world, an Eden or Jerusalem in England's green and pleasant
land. The center of Sidney's civic argument—which I shall analyze
in detail later—is that pagan fictive poetry performs an essential
religious-moral function in allowing men to contemplate that ideal
natural goodness which is like Eden. He draws men toward this
natural goodness by presenting it in the aesthetically attractive
gardens of fiction. Poets write to give men an experience of what it
was to have the natural capacities and the upright reason of the
first garden (Sidney uses the metaphor "divine breath"). His

---

of the Sixteenth Century (London: Warburg, 1948), p. 182, cites an example of its
use in the theory of the Pléiade. Arthur Golding, "Dedication," *the XV bookes of
P. Ovidius Naso entituled Metamorphosis* (1575), fols. A6ᵛ–A7ᵛ, argues that pagan
poets shadowed Christian truths with fables. He reflects a tradition which can be
seen clearly in the multifarious comments on Virgil's fourth Eclogue. Vives and
Landino were proponents of the theory that pagan poets often saw Christian truth
through a glass, darkly. For the humanist tradition that lies behind such comments
on Virgil, see Domenico Comparetti, *Virgil in the Middle Ages*, trans. E. F. M.
Benecke (London, 1895), pp. 96 ff.

6. See W. R. Davis, *Sidney's "Arcadia"* (New Haven: Yale University Press,
1965), pp. 161–167. Davis describes the workings of Sidney's *Arcadia*, and shows
Sidney embodying his theory in fiction. Davis, *Idea*, pp. 31–32, argues that Sidney
thinks of poetry as embodying the noumenal Ideas, as does J. A. Van Dorsten, ed.,
A Defence of Poetry, by Sir Philip Sidney (London: Oxford University Press, 1966),
pp. 11–12, 82–83.

7. Sidney's definition here is like that of San Martino, which Bernard Weinberg
thus characterizes: "One begins, in such a definition, with Aristotle, continues
with Cicero, passes on to Horace, encounters nameless rhetoricians and concludes
with a statement in which all are lumped together" (*A History of Literary Criticism
in the Italian Renaissance* [Chicago: University of Chicago Press, 1961], p. 139).

answer to such men as Blundeville who defended history as the
primary regenerative discipline was that "right poetry" was
superior because it could speak both more precisely and more
movingly of the idea.

Sidney was not, of course, the only writer to present the moral
uses of poetry to his own time. Many of the men with whom he was
acquainted also defended poetry:[8] some of the more literary members of the Leicester circle in England—Spenser, Abraham Fraunce,
Arthur Golding, and Richard Stanihurst; friends and acquaintances
or literary mentors in the Calvinist Huguenot academies in France—
Du Plessis de Mornay and Du Perron; and the members of the
Pléiade in Catholic France—Ronsard, Du Bellay, Pontus de Tyard,
and others. In general, it may be said that Sidney displayed a
deeper understanding of the efficacy of pagan poetry than did the
other defenders of poetry in the Leicester circle; that, though he
adopted the Platonic philosophic posture and epistemology of the
defenders of poetry in the Huguenot, Calvinist academies, he
shifted their emphasis from overtly religious to "right" poetry;
and that, in modifying the theory of inspiration of Du Bellay,
Ronsard, and Pontus de Tyard, the men of the Pléiade, he formu-
lated a defense of "right poetry" which allowed it to exist in its
own right and did not offend the Calvinist with the claim that it
was the result of direct divine inspiration like the Bible.

To turn first to the Leicester circle: while Sidney was composing
the *Defense* (*ca.* 1580–1585), Leicester was one of Elizabeth's more
influential courtiers. To support his Protestant program and to
oppose conservative and Spanish Catholic influence, Leicester
helped finance and support a group of first- and second-rate
writers who developed a body of Protestant and Puritan scholarship, history, theology, polemic, and literature.[9] Dedications to
Leicester suggest that he was interested in historiography which

8. J. A. Van Dorsten, *Poets, Patrons and Professors* (London: Oxford University
Press, 1962), discusses a group of Dutch humanists closely connected with Sidney
and Leicester; Yates, *Academies*, pp. 123–130, *et passim*, discusses the motives and
methods of the Pléiade and the "academy" at the court of Navarre. All these
groups faced the problem of defending secular, as opposed to divine, poetry.

9. Rosenberg, *Leicester*, pp. 11, 37–38, 58, *et passim*.

would bolster the Protestant position, dictionaries and grammars which would help develop a body of learning in the vernacular, and divine poetry of the sort which would fall into Sidney's first class of poetry.[10] Sidney, of course, fits into the program of the Leicester circle. Not only did he write "divine" poetry in his translation of the Psalms, but he also began a translation of Du Bartas's biblically based poem, *The Divine Week*,[11] a poem which promulgated a Protestant teleological view of human history. He began a translation of Du Plessis de Mornay's *Trewenesse*, a work which bent polemic, philosophy, Neo-Platonist humanism, and scriptural interpretation to the confirmation of moderate Protestantism. He did the same sort of literary-religious work as the other writers who sought Leicester's favor, but did it better. And it is possible that the *Defense* was in part an effort to encourage the use of secular poetry as a supplement to the historical studies and translations undertaken by other members of the circle and as an alternative to Bible-based rhyming. Certainly Sidney's connections with Leicester put him in touch with an international group of poets and humanists—mostly Protestants, but including moderate Catholics—who were interested in both politics and letters, and who still retained some of the humane openness and culture of the moderate Catholic French and Italian academies prior to the Saint Bartholomew Massacre (1572).

It was through the Leicester circle that Sidney met Edmund Spenser, who, in his *Shepherd's Calendar* (1579), seems to imply claims for poetry which are quite similar to those which Sidney makes in his *Defense*. It is difficult to speak accurately of Spenser's poetic theory because his critical work, *The English Poet*, has been lost, and we know of it only from E. K.'s glosses to the *Shepherd's Calendar*. All we know for certain of this work is that it would have supported the theory of the poetic frenzy (a theory about which Sidney expressed skepticism); it probably reflected the Neo-Platonist theories of such Pléiade poets as Du Bellay and Pontus de Tyard. However, we can infer some of what Spenser's sense of

10. See *ibid.*, pp. 62–115, for the moral, polemic, and political uses the Leicester circle made of history and historical studies.

11. Joshua Sylvester in Guillaume de Salluste, *Du Bartas, His Divine Weeks and Works*, trans. J. Sylvester (1633), fol. B^v.

poetry's meaning and function must have been at this time from E. K.'s glosses and from the statements about poetry made by the narrative characters in the *Calendar*. For instance, E. K. sets forth an iconological view of poetry in the gloss to "February," and notices the Eustathian allegorical interpretation of the Achilles myth in the note to "March." And Spenser suggests how the ideal world should be embodied in poetry in his fourth Eclogue (one in which he, like Virgil, implies a "golden world"): he makes Colin's shepherdess, Eliza, both the historical Elizabeth and also the immortal mirror of the Idea of beauty. In "October," Spenser portrays in Cuddie a would-be epic poet who cannot find ideal virtue to imitate in the temporal world, and a would-be tragic poet who lacks the wine, poetic frenzy, and ivy which would prompt the high style. If the *Calendar* is a guide, *The English Poet* probably deplored the soul's unfortunate slavery to "the truth of a foolish [temporal] world" and elaborated the poet's function of bodying forth the Ideas of the moral virtues and overtly praising them. In none of this, save in the conception of poetic frenzy, is Spenser very different from Sidney. In any case, Spenser's apparent conception of poetry as a moral art, an allegorical art, and a bodying forth of the noumenal is important to understanding the milieu of the *Defense*.

Other defenders of poetry in Leicester's circle were not so sophisticated. One traditional view current among members of the circle was that much of the poetry, which "lied" according to Plato (and the muse-haters who cited him), was indeed an allegory. The currency of this view was probably useful to Sidney, for one of the jobs which he set himself was to answer Plato's charge.[12] Members of the circle who were reasonably close to Sidney defended poetry as allegory both before and after Sidney worked on the *Defense*. For instance, Abraham Fraunce made such a defense in his *Third Part of the Countess of Pembroke's Ivy-Church* (1592). In it, Fraunce echoes allegorizing mythographers from Fulgentius through Boccaccio to Natalis Comes, and seems to depend immedi-

---

12. For the notion that poets lie, expressed in Renaissance terms, see, e.g., Stephen Gosson, *The School of Abuse* (1579), p. 4; W. A. Ringler, Jr., ed., & W. Allen, trans., *Oratio in Laudem Artis Poeticae*, by John Rainolds (Princeton: Princeton University Press, 1940), p. 71.

ately upon Leone Ebreo's *Dialoghi D'Amore* (1535) for his analytic distinctions.[13] Fraunce explains that poetry is a speaking picture which covers philosophic and Neo-Platonic mysteries with an allegoric veil, and cites the works of Plato and Pythagoras as examples of allegorical mystification. (These "mysteries" and their "veils" were commonplace in commentaries on the *Phaedrus*, *Timaeus*, and *Symposium*.) The same veils and mysteries are, according to Fraunce, the stuff of the Song of Songs (in which opinion he agrees with its Renaissance exegetes such as Martin del Rio). He also says that the purpose of the allegory is to confirm memory, stir up delight, and lure minds, through delight, to the contemplation of divine, astrological, and metaphysical mysteries.[14]

Arthur Golding, a Puritan connected, like Fraunce, with the Leicester circle, uses myth as does Fraunce, and urges many of the same functions for poetic fiction in his translation of Ovid's *Metamorphoses* (1567). He allegorizes Ovid's myths, sometimes philosophically, sometimes morally, and sometimes euhemeristically. He argues that pagan poets foreshadow the Scripture, but hide the truth under veils, and, for example, identifies the "golden age" of Ovid with "Adam's time in Paradise."[15] The Catholic Richard Stanihurst, whom Sidney supported at the university, roughed in approximately the same view of poetry in his translation of Virgil (1582). Finally, to complete our account of the men of the Sidney-Leicester circle, Sir John Harington cites Sidney's *Defense* and develops, in the Preface to his 1591 translation of Ariosto's *Orlando Furioso*,[16] a theory of poetry like Fraunce's. According to Harington, poetry is an allegory composed of a rind which immortalizes great men, an inner pith which offers moral examples to active men, and a kernel which conveys contemplative truth to spiritual men. This tradition of allegorical interpretation is what Sidney refers to when he urges his reader "to believe with Clauserus, the translator of

13. I owe the identification of Fraunce's source, Ebreo, to W. R. Davis.

14. Abraham Fraunce, *The Third Part of the Countess of Pembroke's Ivy-Church* (1592), pp. 3–4.

15. Arthur Golding, "Dedication," *Metamorphosis*, fol. A7^r, identifies the golden age explicitly with prelapsarian Eden.

16. Sir John Harington, trans., *Orlando Furioso* (1591), by Ludovico Ariosto, fol. ¶4^r. See also Edward Fairfaxe, trans., *Godfrey of Bulloigne* (1600), by Torquato Tasso, fols. A2^v–A4^v.

Cornutus, that it pleased the heavenly deity by Hesiod and Homer, under the veil of fables to give us all knowledge . . .; to believe with me that there are many mysteries contained in poetry which of purpose were written darkly lest by profane wits it should be abused." Sidney's *Defense*, however, depends much more than do Fraunce and Harington on the notion that men must be *moved* to virtue; and in leaning on poetry's capacity to move through images he also tends to lean much more upon traditional rhetorical disciplines concerned with "moving" than do they.

The second group of defenders of poetry which Sidney knew or knew of were members of the Calvinistic, Huguenot academies: Du Bartas and Du Plessis de Mornay. Sidney knew, or knew of, these two continental Protestant defenders of poetry through his Leicester connections. Sidney's relationship with Du Plessis de Mornay was so close that Mornay's wife remarked that Sidney and Walsingham were her husband's chief companions in England. His connection with Du Bartas was more tenuous: Du Bartas praised Sidney's poetry, the two had friends in common, and Sidney knew Du Bartas's poetry and translated part of his *Divine Week*. Mornay and Du Bartas set forth a view of the function of poetry more explicitly dependent upon Neo-Platonistic metaphysics than that of Sidney's English contemporaries and associates (with the exception of Spenser).

Much of Mornay's *Trewnesse of the Christian Religion* is an effort to show (as critics had attempted to show from at least Mussato's time) that pagan poets and philosophers foreshadowed the truths of Christianity, and he uses the same allegorical techniques of interpretation as Fraunce, Golding, and Harington. But his concern is deeper and like Sidney's: to give a philosophic and psychological explanation to the "lying" or fictional element in ancient poetry, myth, and philosophy. Mornay may begin with a euhemeristic explanation of a story. The ancient myths are a sort of folk history, "true in that they report deeds rightly beseeming men, untrue in that they attribute them to Gods." [17] His folk history then often

17. Philippe Du Plessis de Mornay, *A Woorke Concerning the Trewnesse of the Christian Religion*, trans. Sir Philip Sidney and Arthur Golding (1587), p. 384; cf. pp. 29–41, 380–396.

develops into an analysis of a set of pagan figures, which are said
to have developed their own power in man's spiritual life by
becoming fictions, myths, or icons which live in the minds of men
and come to inhabit the imagination in ways which do not reflect
their original genesis.[18] Thus Mornay examines the ways in which
devils took over the images of the pagan gods and used their power
in the imagination to corrupt the worship of men (Spenser works
this process out in detail in the Red Cross Knight's Archimago-
induced dream of Venus, and Milton uses it to explain the tempta-
tion of Eve). The devil-inhabited images may become an iconic
path to spiritual destruction; those inhabited by more benign
influences may become a path to moral or metaphysical truth.
Mornay draws many of his interpretations from Neo-Platonic
philosophers such as Iamblicus, and develops Neo-Platonic interpretations of mythic poetry in order to render his images theologically meaningful and metaphysically regenerative. Mornay's
God is Iamblicus's "fountain and root of all . . . forms, shapes or
patterns (conceived or conceivable in mind or imagination)"; his
Orphic poets prefigure the Trinity in describing a creating Jupiter
(power) assisted by Pallas (wisdom) and Love; his Logos is Philo's
"pattern of patterns"; his fall of man, following Plotinus, is imaged
by the soul's fall, through a corruption of the imagination, from the
contemplation of the Idea to the contemplation of matter.[19] Thus,
Mornay interprets many poetic myths as showing aspects of the
noumenal world under the veil of metaphor and allegory, and

18. Emblem books reflected an attempt to develop or employ the semi-magical
powers which hermetists and Neo-Platonists attributed to images and hieroglyphs:
see Mario Praz, *Studies in Seventeenth-Century Imagery*, 2nd ed. (Rome: Edizioni di
Storia, 1964), p. 23; Frances Yates, *Giordano Bruno and the Hermetic Tradition*
(Chicago: University of Chicago Press, 1964), pp. 163–164. E. H. Gombrich,
"*Icones Symbolicae*: The Visual Image in Neo-Platonic Thought," *Journal of the
Warburg Institute*, XI (1948), pp. 163–188, points out the near identity between
emblems and Neo-Platonic Ideas. Emblem books served as a vector for literary
theory also: see Robert J. Clements, *Picta Poesis* (Rome: Edizioni di Storia,
1960), passim. In medieval homiletic tradition springing from Gregory, pictures
or images were, to the laity, what Scripture was to clerks: see G. R. Owst,
Literature and Pulpit in Medieval England, 2nd ed. (Oxford: Blackwell, 1961), pp.
137–138.

19. Mornay, pp. 32, 71–74, 314–315.

relates this ideal truth to Christian truth. He is far more explicitly
Platonic and philosophic than is Fraunce.

Du Bartas developed Mornay's sort of harmony between Neo-
Platonist theory and Christianity,[20] but he also asserted vigorously
an element of Neo-Platonist theory which Sidney wished to deny.
For Du Bartas attributes the poet's ability to perceive the moral
Ideas to *a poetic frenzy*. The poetic frenzy was important in Neo-
Platonist and French poetic theory in the sixteenth century; to it the
theorists attributed the poet's ability to perceive supernatural and
ideal truth. Indeed, all of the members of the academy at the court
of Navarre, Huguenots whom Sidney knew or knew of (Du Bartas,
Mornay, Agrippa D'Aubigne and Hotman), emphasized the frenzy
that accompanied or caused poetic inspiration. Since the members
of the academy at Navarre also developed a program for humane
learning much like that of the Leicester circle—divine poetry,
vernacular Psalms, learned translations,[21]—Sidney's difference from
them in the matter of the poetic frenzy is the more significant.

The third group of defenders of poetry with which I should like to
compare Sidney are the Pléiade poets: Ronsard, Du Bellay, Pontus
de Tyard, Baïf, Dorat. These moderate Catholic academicians were
not only defenders of poetry; they were poets interested in religious
reconciliation throughout Europe. They, like Sidney, were interested
in using art to help build the just commonwealth. Sidney certainly
knew of their poetry through Spenser; he may have known their
theoretical discussions directly from his 1572 residence in Paris; or he
may have known of the discussions indirectly through his friends
Languet and Buchanan. What the men of the Pléiade did in
defending poetry was essentially to claim the same sorts of functions
for it as did Sidney. But they also claimed too much for poetry,
asserting, like the Navarre group, that it is "inspired" and that it
acts to raise one to Heaven. Sidney both limits the sense in which
poetry is inspired and denies it the power to redeem.

Ronsard, Du Bellay, and Pontus de Tyard—the chief of the

---

20. *Du Bartas*, pp. 53–54, 87. For a discussion of Du Bartas's Platonism, see
G. S. Du Bartas, *Works*, ed. U. T. Holmes, *et al*. (Chapel Hill: University of North
Carolina Press, 1935), I, 139–141.

21. Yates, *Academies*, pp. 114–116, 152, 265.

Pléiade's defenders of the poetic frenzy—all incorporate the frenzy of inspiration into their poetic theory, but Tyard discusses it in greater detail than do Du Bellay and Ronsard. Tyard speaks of the frenzy almost as if it were a spirit which possesses the poet's soul. This frenzy clears the eyes of his mind of material phantasms and of the deceptions of the senses, and lifts him to within sight of the moral Ideas, so that he sees them and can imitate them. His frenzy communicates itself to his readers, who also, to a lesser degree, are enabled by it to contemplate the Ideas.[22] The poetic frenzy becomes in Tyard similar to possession by the Holy Ghost. Du Bellay implicitly extends the process initiated by poetic frenzy; he suggests that the contemplation of the Ideas (made possible by the frenzy according to Tyard) is a stage in the salvation of the soul:

Within the cloister of the mysterious Ideas,
From the large troop of immortal souls
The Fore-knower has chosen the most beautiful
To be guided, through Himself, to Himself,
So that, little by little, they are hoisted toward the heavens
Upon the pulley of their divine wings,
Flying to the bosom of Eternal beauty,
Where they are cleansed of all vice.
The Just alone justifies His elect,
Restores them to their primal life,
And makes them almost equal His Son.[23]

22. Grahame Castor, *Pléiade Poetics* (Cambridge: Cambridge University Press, 1964), pp. 31–33.

23. Joachim Du Bellay, "Olive," no. cxii, in *Poesies*, ed. E. Courbet (Paris: Garnier, 1918), I, 67:

> Dedans le close des occultes Idées,
> Au grand troupeau des ames immortelles,
> Le Prevoyant a choisi les plus belles,
> Pour estre à luy par luymesme guidées
> Lors peu à peu devers le ciel guindées
> Dessus l'engin de leurs divines aeles,
> Vollent au seing des beautez aeternelles,
> Ou elle'sont de tout vice emendées.
> Le Juste seul ses eleuz justifie,
> Les reanime en leur premiere vie,
> Et à son filz les faict quasi egaulz.

The defenders of poetic fiction in England when set against believers in such an exalted Platonism may seem a bit drab. The Pléiade Neo-Platonists, however, would have seemed a bit theologically careless to the English Puritans. Poetry, as outlined by Du Bellay and Tyard, seems able to do what Calvin's Christ is able to do. The poet's frenzy seems indistinguishable from the inspiration which created the Psalms. The poetry which lifts the reader to perceive the Ideas directly and places him before the throne of God seems to parallel, in its power, the action of the Holy Ghost.

One may define a critic by his differentia, as well as by his genus. Sidney does not choose to venture onto the thin metaphysical ice which underlay the Pléiade's theory of the poetic frenzy. Although he invites the reader to believe with Landino, the fifteenth-century Florentine Platonic academy's commentator on Virgil and Dante, that poets are inspired by a divine frenzy, he does not suggest that to believe with Landino is also to believe with Sidney. He has earlier denied belief in the poetic fury. He says that Plato attributes to poetry "more then myself do, namely to be a very inspiring of a divine force, far above man's wit." He also denies his assent to the theory of the poet's frenzy in *Astrophel and Stella*:

> Some do I here of Poet's furie tell
> But (God wot) wot not what they meane by it.[24]

(In this same sonnet he, like Persius, also denies drinking from Aganippe's well, or sleeping on Helicon.) In the *Defense*, Sidney substitutes for the theologically dubious "divine frenzy" the theologically sound "divine breath" as the poet's inspiration. By this substitution Sidney makes a crucial break with those who wrote Neo-Platonist defenses of poetry in his milieu and time, men who had claimed, as he did, that poetry is allegorical, fictive, an embodiment of the Ideas, and regenerative.

Sidney's conception of the divine breath which inspires a poet and clears his inner eyes is a conception of a breath which works like the inbreathed gift which Adam received. It is a *natural gift*, one given under natural law (not a supernatural gift beyond human potentiality and granted by a special grace). As a result of this natural gift,

24. Sir Philip Sidney, "Astrophel and Stella," no. lxxiv, ll. 5–7, in *Poems*, ed. W. A. Ringler, Jr. (Oxford: Clarendon Press, 1962), p. 204; see also p. 480 n.

the poet creates a "golden world" like the natural Paradise in which Adam lived before he broke his lease. If "right" poetry springs from a natural, if uncorrupt, source, its embodiment of the moral Ideas also leads toward a natural, prelapsarian, innocence. This innocence is not in Renaissance theological terms the perfection of Heaven. Natural law and reason (the divine breath) require justice, prudence, temperance, and fortitude; they forward the virtues of the just secular citizen and householder. They do not inspire faith, hope, or love; and Sidney does not argue that classical poets develop these virtues.

Sidney thus differentiates between the work of the poet and the work of the prophet. The poet does not save men; he merely habituates them to the Eden they would have lived in had not Adam fallen, and accustoms them to experience, love, and enact virtue. Salvation comes through Christ; poetry merely aids in recovering some of Adam's primal natural virtue. Poetry can help man model himself on uncorrupt natural Adam; it does not make it possible for him to imitate Christ. By this careful differentiation of function, Sidney made a place for fiction and poetry in a Protestant universe. The poet does not claim to be a prophet, a preacher, or a vessel of salvation.

The central theses of Sidney's theory of poetry are contained in the following sentences from the *Defense*:

> There is no art delivered unto mankind that has not the works of nature for his principal object . . . .

> [Nature's] world is brazen, the poets only deliver a golden.

> Only the poet, disdaining to be tied to any such subjection [to the fallen second nature of the temporal world], lifted up with the vigor of his own invention, does grow in effect into another nature [prelapsarian Eden inhabited by the Ideas of the virtues] in making things either better than nature brings forth or, quite anew, forms such as never were in nature, as the heroes, demigods, cyclops, chimeras, furies, and such-like.

> The skill of each artificer stands in that Idea or fore-conceit of the work, and not in the work itself, and that the poet has that Idea [that he has perceived the ideal world: Eden, the golden world] is manifest by [his] delivering them forth in such excellency as he had imagined

them. Which delivering forth also is not wholly imaginative (as we are wont to say by them that build castles in the air) but so far substantially it works, not only to make a Cyrus (which had been but a particular excellence as nature might have done) but to bestow a Cyrus upon the world to make many Cyruses, if they will learn aright why and how that maker made him.

[God] set [man] beyond and over all the works of that second [post-lapsarian] nature, which in nothing he shows so much as in poetry, when with the force of a divine breath he brings things forth far surpassing her doings [ideas embodied from the first, or prelapsarian, nature] (with no small argument to the incredulous of that first accursed fall of Adam, since our erected wit makes us know what perfection is and yet our infected will keeps us from reaching unto it).

Running through these passages is a reference to two natures: one physical, natural, perceptible to our senses, the stage of human history since Adam; the other a nature "above nature," a "golden world" which manifests "perfection." It is possible to interpret Sidney to mean that the poet imagines a world for the reader which is simply less frustrating than the one he experiences daily, a sort of secular escape into fantasy. However, Sidney prevents us from seeing poetry merely as the tranquilizer of the intellect by asserting that the poet's "delivering forth . . . is not wholly imaginative," not the building of "castles in the air." The poet imitates "what may be and ought to be," and his imitation is above nature in the sense that it delivers forth embodiments of the moral Ideas. The poet re-creates, in fact, Marsilio Ficino's world of metaphysical Ideas.[25] Sidney argues that the poet's wit evidences Adam's fall by making us know what perfection is, and thus presents a variant of Anselm's

25. The Neo-Platonist commonplace of a nature in which the Ideas exist could have come to Sidney through many sources. The most immediate is Mornay, *Trewnesse*, pp. 149–152 and 70–75, where first, or prelapsarian, nature is eternal, and second, or postlapsarian, nature is temporal and subject to change. Scaliger, *Poetices libri septem*, I, i, is another possible source: see Marvin Herrick, *The Fusion of Horatian and Aristotelian Criticism, 1531–1555*, Illinois Studies in Language and Literature, vol. XXXII, no. 1 (Urbana, 1946), p. 26. Ficino identifies the world of men before the fall with the realm of Ideas in his commentary on the Symposium: Marsilio Ficino, *Commentary on Plato's Symposium*, ed. & trans. Sears R. Jayne, University of Missouri Studies, vol. XIX, no. 1 (Columbia, 1944), pp. 155–156. See also André Chastel, *Art et Humanisme à Florence au Temps de Laurent le Magnifique* (Paris: French University Presses, 1961), p. 201.

argument for the existence of God as an explanation of the function of poetry.

Sidney's use of "Idea" may seem ambiguous, for he may be interpreted to suggest that the "Idea" or "fore-conceit" of the work is the plan of the work. The "fore-conceit" or "Idea" which the poet has in mind, and which determines the intrinsic excellence of the work is, however, not the technical plan for achieving successful imitation, but rather the perception of the Idea which the poet imitates. The "fore-conceit" becomes, like the Platonic Ideas in Spenser's Garden of Adonis, a pattern informing the "clay" or substance of mortal, postlapsarian nature. The Idea informs the clay, and remakes individuals through the pattern presented as a compelling experience in poetry; the experience of the Ideal Cyrus makes it possible for men to model themselves upon the Idea Cyrus embodies. The first nature, an uncorrupt nature before the fall of man, contains forms or Ideas in their uncorrupt natural perfection. The "fore-conceit" is the poet's perception of this potential perfection; the fore-conceit has become a Pisgah-sight of the Platonic Ideas inhabiting Eden before man corrupted nature. The "force of a divine breath," what God breathed into Adam (his soul or reason), permits the "right poet," who has cleared the eyes of his mind by faith, to exercise his natural reason so that he can perceive the Ideas of the virtues. He then proceeds to imitate these. "Right poetry" does not ravish the soul to the Throne of God, where she stands overwhelmed and adoring perforce; rather it leads the soul, using natural passion and reason (and assuming faith) to Eden, where she finds Ideas which work substantially to create excellent individuals, given the condition that the Ideas are imitated in words duly ordered. Our erected wit can contemplate the Ideas; the experience of the golden world helps change our corrupted will.

Ordering words duly was the province of human wit and the art of rhetoric. Sidney uses the prosaic capabilities of rhetoric, those assumed in Quintilian and Cicero, in countless imitators, and in commentators on Horace, to show how the poet can, using human and natural capabilities, create for his audience the experience of the Ideas he perceives. The French Neo-Platonist theorists had argued that the poet transmits his divine frenzy to his audience, and that it is this frenzy which "strikes, pierces, and possesses" the soul of the audience and lifts it to contemplate Ideas. Du Bartas compares the poet's power to a seal impressing its form on hot wax:

> And, as a Seal printed in wax (almost)
> Another Seal; a learned *Poet* graveth
> So deep his passions in his Readers Ghost,
> That oft the Reader th'Authors form receiveth,
> For, Verses vertue, sliding secretly
> (By secret Pipes) through th'*intellectuall Notions;*
> Of all that's pourtraid artificially
> Imprenteth there both good and evill motions.[26]

Du Bartas has in mind the rhetorical power of *enargeia*, or vividness, a power which Dekker says transmits the author's frenzy to the actor, who, employing the rhetorical skills of delivery, transmits the passion to the audience in his turn:

> That Man give mee, whose brest filled by the *Muses,*
> With Raptures, Into a second, them infuses:
> Can give an Actor, Sorrow, Rage, Joy, Passion,
> Whilst hee againe (by self-same Agitation)
> Commands the *Hearers,* sometimes drawing out teares,
> Then smiles, and fills them both with *Hopes* and *Feares.*[27]

Both Dekker and Du Bartas mingle the spiritual power of the poetic frenzy, or rapture, and the technical rhetorical power of *enargeia*

---

26. *Du Bartas,* p. 242.

27. Thomas Dekker, "Prologue," ll. 37–42, to *If This Be Not a Good Play,* in *The Dramatic Works,* ed. F. Bowers (Cambridge: Cambridge University Press, 1953–1961), III, 122. For a discussion of the importance of the concept of *enargeia* in Sidney's fiction and poetry, see Neil L. Rudenstine, *Sidney's Poetic Development* (Cambridge, Mass.: Harvard University Press, 1967) pp. 149–171. The concept sprang from Ciceronian and rhetorical theorizing; the Italian Neo-Platonists elaborated it. See Baxter Hathaway, *The Age of Criticism* (Ithaca: Cornell University Press, 1962), pp. 10–12, 190–191, 201–202, for a discussion of the importance the concept assumed in Italian theories of imitation. He lists the major critical discussions on p. 12. *Enargeia* also remained vital in rhetorical training for orators and actors, and participated in the ambiguity surrounding imitation through words, and imitation through gesture and expression. See B. L. Joseph, *Elizabethan Acting* (Oxford University Press, 1951), pp. 62–72, and W. S. Howell, *Logic and Rhetoric in England: 1500–1700* (Princeton: Princeton University Press, 1956) pp. 121, 127, for a discussion of its relation to delivery, and the distinction between *Energia* and *Enargeia.*

and delivery to create a lively experience for the audience. Sidney does away with the notion that a poem automatically transmits the poet's special powers or experiences. He argues instead that these can be transmitted only by the poet's undergoing the discipline of a natural, technical study, the study of rhetoric. This power could, for example, set a boiling pot before an audience, according to rhetoricians; it can also, according to Sidney, recreate the poet's experience of the Ideas for the audience.

The transmission of the poetic frenzy, and its metaphysical effects as envisaged by the French Neo-Platonists, closely paralleled the action attributed to the Psalms by many commentators.[28] Sidney wishes to distinguish between the Divine poetry characteristic of the Psalms and "right" poetry. By attributing the poet's power of transmission to rhetoric, and of perception to reason, Sidney again makes the poet the good citizen and frees him of the burdens of prophecy and scripture which would exile him from a Puritan commonwealth.

Sidney chose to develop his theory of poetry in a "Defense," a rhetorical genre familiar both to the Renaissance critic and to the Renaissance schoolboy. Sidney's *Defense* is only one of many defenses which humanists had written in praise of everything from poetry to poverty, and which schoolmasters had forced schoolboys to write in order to teach them to invent and organize. Sidney organized his *Defense* according to a standard rhetorical scheme.[29] The typical defense, as every schoolboy who had read Thomas Wilson's *Arte of Rhetorique* (1553) knew, contained seven parts: the *exordium*, the *narratio*, the *partitio*, the *propositio*, the *confirmatio*, the *reprehensio*, and the *peroratio*.[30] Sidney adds a *digressio*.

28. See, e.g., John Calvin, *The Psalms with John Calvins Commentary*, trans. Arthur Golding (1571), fols. *4ᵛ–*8ᵛ; Immanuel Tremellius and Franciscus Junius, "Preface," in *Bibliorum Pars Tertia* (1580), p. 4.

29. I base this discussion of the form of the *Defense* on K. O. Myrick, *Sir Philip Sidney as a Literary Craftsman*, 2nd ed. (Lincoln: University of Nebraska Press, 1965), pp. 46–83. For an analysis which emphasizes the ramistic influence on the form of the *Defense*, see G. W. Hallam, "Sidney's Supposed Ramism," *Renaissance Papers 1963* (Durham: Southeastern Renaissance Conference, 1964), pp. 12–17.

30. Thomas Wilson, *The Arte of Rhetorique (1553)*, ed. R. Bowers (Gainesville, Fla.: Scholars Reprints, 1962), p. 127.

Sidney begins his *Defense* with an introduction (*exordium*) which uses the pleasant tale recommended by Wilson to win the good will of the audience. He follows with a statement of the problem at issue (*narratio*), one having to do with the moral character of the poet and the effects of poetry. In his definition of the issue (*propositio*) he tries to give "the sum of the whole matter" by defining Poetry: "Poetry therefore is an Art of imitation, for so Aristotle terms it in the word *mimesis*, that is to say a representing, counterfeiting, or figuring forth (to speak metaphorically, a speaking picture) with this end, to teach and delight."

In his analysis of the relevant arguments (*partitio*), he first tells us that he will not deal with poets who "imitate the inconceivable excellencies of God," since his Puritan audience could hardly object to divine poetry, nor will he deal with the philosophic poet. In the second section of the *partitio*, he gives examples of how "right" poetry permits the reader to experience "notable images of virtues [and] vices." Sidney has defined his relevant arguments as those arguments relating to the moral effect of poetry, and it is at this point that he gives a number of implicit exegeses of classical and biblical fictions which reveal his notion of how poetry sets forth a paradigm drawn from the golden world of first nature, and clothes the paradigm in particulars drawn from the sensible, material, postlapsarian world of second nature.

These exegeses may be set beside those of Spenser and E. K. mentioned earlier (or beside Fraunce's exegeses of Venus and Cupid as expressing the Idea of the corrupted generative power in man,[31] or Harington's exegesis of Atlante and his horse as, like Cupid, embodying a speaking picture of the Idea of lust).[32] Sidney's comments make the heroes of classical poems speaking pictures of vices and virtues in much the same way that the personified abstractions of Caesario Ripa's *Iconologia* are pictures of the Ideas of the virtues and vices; he almost says "If you want to experience the vices, try Ajax as anger, Agamemnon as pride, Gnatho and Pandar as lust, Eteocles and Polynices as ambition. If you wish to experience virtue, try Ulysses for wisdom, Diomedes for temperance, Achilles for

31. Fraunce, *Ivy-Church*, fols. 39^{r-v}, 45^v–46^r.
32. Harington, *Orlando*, p. 30.

fortitude, or Xenophon's Cyrus for justice." He extends his treatment of fiction as embodying speaking pictures of the Ideas of the virtues to divine poetry; Dives and Lazarus become pictures of the Ideas of uncharitableness and humility; the prodigal and his father—who in modern exegesis become the soul and God—are for Sidney primarily pictures of the Ideas of disobedience and of mercy. Appropriately, Sidney seems to see theological virtues pictured in the Parables, and moral virtues pictured in right poetry.

Sidney does not care whether his speaking pictures of the Ideas are historical, exemplary, or allegorical embodiments of the Idea. A Parable will do as well as history in verse; Aesop's animals will do, and so will Virgil's Aeneas; Dante's visit to an imagined world will do, and so will Xenophon's narration of purportedly accurate history. A mythic Tantalus can say as much as a historical Cyrus, or a half-historical Ulysses. The garden of Sidney's golden world is filled with historical and figurative icons, speaking pictures of the Ideas and Patterns according to which men must more or less conform themselves, and which inform our concept of what is possible to humanity.

In his proof (*confirmatio*), Sidney defines the purpose of learning in terms which would assign it an important role in man's recovery from what Mornay and the Neo-Platonists pictured as the fall of man. All learning draws man to as high a perfection as his degenerate, clay-clogged soul can glimpse. Since the contemplative sciences of the quadrivium result in knowing (*gnosis*), not necessarily in doing (*praxis*), Sidney turns to the moral sciences, sciences which explicitly intend to inspire both knowledge of the ideal and those actions necessary to realize this ideal as much as possible in the corrupt world of second nature. Philosophy, poetry, and history had all claimed to teach ideal virtue to encourage virtuous action; Sidney considers their claims.

He first attacks the forbidding abstraction of the teaching given in ethics, and prepares his ground both for his attack on history's slavery to the imperfect particular, and for his defense of poetry, which can combine the vivid particular with the general truth. Philosophy is all paradigm and precept, history all concrete and flawed example. Sidney, to win his case, need only show in his proof

that the poet can present a picture of virtue which is more easily
and vividly experienced than that of the philosopher, and one less
corrupted by vicious particularities than that of the historian. He
does so. His poet gives both the precept and the example; he gives
life and breath to a perfect precept, and gives the perfection of
precept to speaking examples.

In the second section of his proof, Sidney disciplines the classical
theory of the genres to the service of his general theory. He subordinates the formal description of each genre to its moral function,
and treats the genres as a series of graded steps to beatitude. He
begins with the humble and allegorical experience offered by the
pastoral, in which Meliboeus tells of tyrants' rule and Tityrus of
benevolence, wolves embody wrongdoing and sheep patience. He
moves to the modified rapture offered by the elegy, which embodies
weakness and wretchedness and so awakens just compassion. He
proceeds to satire and its embodiment of the shame accompanying
vice, and then to comedy which embodies the negative and ironic
wisdom which enables us to recognize everyday folly. He continues
with tragedy, which embodies the exalted, pathetic, and self-
punished pride that Lear's fool sees in Lear, or Seneca sees in
Oedipus. He moves finally to the analysis of those genres which
embody the noblest *eidola:* the lyric and heroic poems. Since the
lyric praises the virtues and God, its art moves the heart more than
does a trumpet. His description of the metaphysical ecstasy created
by the heroic poem (which "does not only teach and move to a
truth, but teaches and moves to the most high and excellent truth"
and "makes magnanimity and justice shine through all misty
fearfulness and foggy desires") reveals that Sidney understands the
delight appropriate to the heroic *eidolon* to be the ecstasy of the
Neo-Platonist confronted with the veiled Ideas of virtue, the delight
of those who, if they "could see virtue would be wonderfully
ravished with the love of her beauty." The delight which Sidney's
genres offer at their best is both the rhetorical delight in a sugared
invention—a tale "which holds children from play and old men
from the chimney corner"—and the moral delight of an ecstatic
vision of perfect virtue at liberty in a golden Eden. There is, ultimately, no bitterness in Sidney's medicine of cherries; there are only

two kinds of delight. In the series of graded steps to beatitude and magnanimity supplied by the genres, both kinds of delight aim at one end, the beginnings of regeneration through the experience of the golden world inhabited by the Ideas of the virtues and imitated by the poet.

Sidney summarizes his proof, and then moves into his refutation of opposing arguments (*reprehensio*); he refutes the stock arguments of the poet-haters and develops once more, by negative definition this time, his theory of the method by which poets create for their readers an experience of the golden world. He parries the first argument, that poetry is a waste of time, by definition. He deals more carefully with the second attack, that poets are liars, by using the deliberately shocking and paradoxical form of argument made most familiar by Cornelius Agrippa.[33] He demonstrates the vanity and incertitude of history. He points out that poets cannot lie, for they affirm nothing as fact, while historians must affirm as fact statements which can never, in the cloudy knowledge of mankind, be known as certain: "If then a man can arrive to the child's age to know that the poets' persons and doings are but pictures what should be [i.e., the ethically possible], and not stories what have been, they will never give the lie to things not affirmatively, but allegorically and figuratively written."

Sidney then gives examples of the poet's moral work which suggest a medieval argument against the attack that the poet's works are lies, an argument which discriminated levels of statement on the basis of whether they concerned "fable," "argument," or "history." All of these levels of discourse allowed for meaningful reshaping of material drawn from the fallen world of second nature. The lying fable, neither true nor true-seeming, reshaped its material as allegory; the lying argument, not true, but true-seeming, developed examples, as in comedies; but history, which strove for truth and was true seeming, developed its examples in histories, in parts of the epics, and in tragedies. Sidney finds more useful a somewhat similar argument against the charge of lying which discriminated levels of discourse through the use of a set of terms popular among Italian critics during the 1580s: the terms "icastic" and "fantastic"

33. Hamilton, *Structure*, pp. 18 ff.

which came originally from Plato's discussion of painting in *Sophist* 235–236. Plato uses "icastic" to mean the *trompe d'oeil* reproduction of material fact, and "fantastic" to mean the depiction of fictitious mental images. For Plato, material fact exists at at least one remove from noumenal reality. A mental image is, therefore, a distortion of a material fact. An "icastic" imitation exists at two removes from noumenal reality. A "fantastic" imitation exists at three or four removes. Moreover, a "fantastic" imitation is, for Plato, synonymous with deliberate lying. The modern use of the terms which makes the icastic imitator the master of useful, civilization-building fictions may have begun with Mazzoni and Tasso, who paired them in their argument (*ca.* 1580–1594) over the nature of the heroic poem. The final form of their argument came out only after Sidney's death, but the discussion had been going on earlier,[34] and Spenser's knowledge of Tasso and his critical theory, and Spenser's friendship with Sidney, suggest that the distinctions being worked out by Tasso may have informed Sidney's use of the terms. In any case, Tasso's distinctions are similar to Sidney's. His fantastic poet, like the sophist, imitates the apparently probable: he uses equivocations, fallacious logic, and the other deceptive devices useful to the unscrupulous orator; his icastic poet imitates, not material fact, but the probable, the verisimilar, the universal, and the intelligible. His fantastic poet imitates equivocally the sensible; his icastic poet imitates the true, which is roughly co-terminous with the good. In practical terms, Tasso argues that the icastic poet imitates the truths of religion, science, and morality by embodying them in such verisimilar pictures as Aeneas.

Having argued that the poet imitates the universal ,and thus cannot lie, Sidney moves to a digression (*digressio*) in the most approved rhetorical style. He uses the digression, as it should be used according to rhetoricians, to discuss something appropriate to the subject but not immediately relevant to the case under judgment, by setting forth a section on practical criticism of English poetry.

Sidney's judgments have been accused of harshness. One should

34. Ettore Mazzali, ed., *Prose*, by Torquato Tasso (Milan: R. Ricciardi, 1959), pp. 487 ff. See G. Shepherd, ed., *An Apology for Poetry*, by Sir Philip Sidney (London: Nelson, 1965), pp. 223–225, for an extensive discussion of Sidney's sources.

remember, however, that when Sidney wrote, Shakespeare had written nothing, and Spenser had in effect, written only the *Shepherd's Calendar*. Of the great poetry of the English Renaissance, only Gascoigne's, Wyatt's, and Surrey's was really available. Drama had not yet supplied those works which triumphed over criticism. Thus Sidney considers an impoverished and sometimes grotesque native heritage. He confidently affirms its future, and this affirmation is more important than the critical narrowness of the passages in which he suggests binding poetry in neoclassical chains. It is of less significance, for instance, that he suggested that the iron unities of time and place be clenched on the drama, than that he confidently asserted that there would be a drama worth shackling. His discussion of the lumbering fourteeners and florid experimental exercises of his contemporaries and immediate forerunners leads him to turn from exalted theory to the more rhetorical or Horatian business of competence. Sidney attempts to develop a brief "Art" of English poetry, a systematized body of precepts which will suggest to the aspiring English poet practical techniques whereby he can imitate the golden world, and practically useful models whose imitations of the golden world he can follow. Here he deals with the standard "art" of poetry, that body of received doctrine and practice which can be taught systematically. As he says, "Daedalus . . . has three wings to bear itself up into the air of due commendation: that is, art, imitation, and exercise." "Imitation" here means the following of models, the copying of a competent poet, a practice recommended in the Horatian and rhetorical commentaries in the Renaissance, and the practical basis of the cultural program of the Pléiade.

A self-imposed apprenticeship to a model poet (which is what Sidney means by "imitation" throughout his digression) is the key to the program Sidney outlines for the enrichment of English poetry. Since both critical doctrine and imitation are necessary to the poet, his practical recommendations must be of two sorts. He must first name English poets skilful enough to act as models for aspiring poets, and he must estimate their strengths and weaknesses as models in accord with a system of "artificial rules" which imply systematic and rational criticism. He can suggest this system without filling in its details, for his system does not differ markedly from the commonplaces rooted in the rhetoricians, embedded in commentaries on Horace, and elaborated by the more neoclassical members of the Pléiade.

When Sidney praises model authors, he praises them almost as if they were manifestations of an Idea: Chaucer is Clarity; Surrey, Nobility; and Spenser, Worthiness itself. When Sidney reprehends, he reprehends according to rhetorical good sense. Spenser's fault is his archaic diction; *Gorboduc* is excellent in conception but unworthy of imitation in detail, since it violates the critics' rule of thumb about unified time and place. Moreover, most English poetry can be condemned by a rhetorician's rule of thumb (which Dante had dignified by including it in the *Vita Nuova*): if a poem cannot be sensibly paraphrased in prose, it will be found that "one verse did but beget another," and the poem is merely an ill-disposed lump of words, tinkling to rhyme, and stuck over with the paper flowers of rhetoric.

In his practical comments on comedy, Sidney returns to his defense of poetry on general moral grounds since he finds, apparently, no native comedies worth discussing as models. (George Gascoigne's *Supposes* [1566], which would satisfy his technical demands, apparently disqualifies because it is a translation of Ariosto's Italian *I Suppositi*.) Critics of poetry had charged that comedy encourages immorality by presenting immoral actions on stage. In defense, Sidney uses a distinction between laughter and delight which springs from Aristotle's *Ethics* (IV, 8) and Cicero's *De Oratore* (II, 58–70), and permeates such Renaissance discussions as Trissino's *Poetica* (IV) and Pontanus' *De Sermone* (III, 22–IV, 4). Laughter arises from the ridiculous, expresses scorn, and is for Sidney an agent of negative moral teaching, for laughter makes men scorn the morally deformed characters who participate in comic action. Comic delight, on the other hand, becomes the agent of positive moral teaching, and arises from the experience of "things that have a conveniency to ourselves or to the general nature." Delight arises from the experience of universals, the Ideas of the good: fair proportions, good chances, the happiness of friends and country. All these examples point to that ecstasy in the presence of the experienced, embodied Idea which Sidney attributes to the golden world. Sidney, like Trissino, points his case with the observation that one might very well be delighted with the sight of a beautiful woman, but one would hardly be moved to laughter.

Sidney also deals with the grammar, rhetoric, and prosody of the English language. He, like Du Bartas, finds that language good which is capable of forming combined words.[35] He has in mind the combined words and epithets to be found in classical and biblical poetry. He argues that, from its linguistic characteristics, one can conclude that English is as capable of imitations of the golden world, and of clarity, elevation, and grace in this imitation, as any language.

Sidney closes his defense with a *peroratio* written in the same easy and graceful tone with which he began. He urges his readers to believe his defense of poetry, and to believe other defenses of poetry, and the arguments presented in them, which sometimes differ from his:

> . . . I conjure you all that have had the evil luck to read this ink-wasting toy of mine, even in the name of the nine Muses, no more to scorn the sacred mysteries of poesy; no more to laugh at the name of poets as though they were next inheritors to fools; no more to jest at the reverent title of a rhymer, but to believe with Aristotle that they were the ancient treasurers of the Grecians' divinity; to believe with Bembus that they were first bringers-in of all civility; to believe with Scaliger that no philosopher's precepts can sooner make you an honest man than the reading of Virgil; to believe with Clauserus, the translator of Cornutus, that it pleased the heavenly Deity, by Hesiod and Homer, under the veil of fables to give us all knowledge, logic, rhetoric, philosophy natural and moral (and what not?); to believe with me that there are many mysteries contained in poetry which of purpose were written darkly lest by profane wits it should be abused; to believe with Landino that they are so beloved of the gods that whatsoever they write proceeds of a divine fury; lastly, to believe themselves when they tell you they will make you immortal by their verses.

35. For a discussion of the partisans of compound words, and their reasons for enthusiasm, see Du Bartas, *Works*, ed. U. T. Holmes, I, 174–175. Tyndale, like Sidney, believed that English was similar to Hebrew and Greek; see J. W. H. Atkins, *English Literary Criticism, The Renascence* (London: Methuen, 1947), p. 97.

Sidney's eclectic sympathies in his peroration fit his program and his tone admirably. In his *Defense*, he wants to win his audience to sympathy with his argument for poetry. He avoids novelty of phrasing. He cites authority, he paraphrases commonplaces, and he writes in the forensic, not in the grand or middle styles. He adds unity and coherence to his citations of authority, and an easy courtly elegance to pedagogic and pedantic commonplaces. But the commonplaces and authorities provided him with one of his most important rhetorical effects, for they enable him to sound everywhere as though he were suggesting nothing novel. He presents what everyone would have recognized as natural and dresses it to advantage.

Sidney subordinates his critical structure (built of commonplaces which concealed the novelty of his basic conception of the function of poetry, supported by authorities who drew attention from the audacity of his synthesis, and presented in an easy style which makes his elevation of aim seem homely and familiar) to an end that Protestant humanists in England and on the Continent had assigned to Divine poetry. He avoids some of the difficulties inherent in their program by rejecting the notion of substituting biblical for secular poetry, and by rejecting the notion of the poet's frenzy. He can thus find a use for fiction (which is what he means by poetry) and yet not attempt to claim parity for it with narrative inspired by the Holy Spirit.

Protestant commentators on the Psalms had emphasized the striking, piercing, and possessing power of David's poetry. Tremellius and Junius had attributed an almost complete program of moral regeneration to the practice of singing Psalms and succumbing to their ravishing power.[36] Sidney may have found a sort of secular analogue to the power of the Psalms in Pythagorean and Neo-Platonist theorizing about the power of music, the harmony of the universe, and the perception of Ideas. These attributions of power to poetry help Sidney direct secular fiction to the imitation of Ideas, to the experience of the golden world of Eden, and to regeneration. Poetry's inspiration is contingent, coming through right reason and natural talent; if it imitates a world unfallen, it

36. Tremellius and Junius, "Preface."

still imitates a natural world. Sidney thus makes room in a Protestant Zion for the poet as well as the Psalmist.

After we have talked of Sidney's sources, after we have recognized his commonplaces, after we have traced his purpose to religion and his form to the schoolroom, we must still recognize the informing spirit, sober, graceful, and amused, which whisks the dust from dry distinctions and overblown commonplaces. Sidney's style reflects the man. His courtly *sprezzatura*, his wit void of pride makes the modern reader experience his humane vision even if he cannot always catalogue its sources. His style, flexible enough for art, conscious enough of its own art to sport with art, can speak of the exalted work of regenerating the sons of Adam, or the humble drudgery of counting syllables without losing its easy grace and good sense. It is a style which draws us to like the advocate and love his cause. If the poet habituates us to the golden world, Sidney habituates us to walking there easily yet modestly, and to accepting a concept of poetry which Spenser might have used to help envisage his great work of building a Zion in England, a concept which Milton would have thought appropriate to describe his own great argument.

A Note on the Text of this Edition

Sidney's *Defense of Poesy* has been "many times printed and edited, but never with an accurate text." [37] This lack of precision results from the existence of two versions of the text drawn from independent manuscripts. [38] The principal sources that must be collated or consulted to establish a text differ among themselves in over four hundred particulars. There are two printed primary sources for Sidney's work: *An Apology for Poetry* (1595), STC 22534, printed for Henry Olney, and *The Defence of Poesie* (1595), STC 22535, printed for William Ponsonby. There is another quarto, *The Defence of Poesie* (1595), STC 22534+, which consists of the Olney sheets bound with a Ponsonby title page.

37. W. A. Ringler, Jr., "Master Drant's Rules," *Philological Quarterly*, XXIX (1950), p. 73. This lack of an accurate text will be supplied when Professor William Elwood's forthcoming definitive edition of the *Apology* is published.

38. W. H. Bond, "The Bibliographical Jungle," *Times Literary Supplement*, September 23, 1949, p. 624.

Three manuscript sources help the study of the text. The Penshurst manuscript apparently belonged to Sidney's brother, Robert. Sidney's secretary, William Temple, quotes from an *Apology* in his "*Analysis tractationis de poesi*" (1584) (De Lisle and Dudley MS 1095). Professor Mary Mahl has recently discovered and edited the Norwich manuscript which seems to represent an earlier state of Olney's copy-text than any we have had heretofore.[39] All three of these manuscripts seem to be related to the Olney copy-text. The Penshurst manuscript contains some corrections and corruptions drawn from a source related to the Ponsonby copy-text, but it seems to be at least a tertiary form of the text Olney used for his edition.

Since the *Apology* and the *Defense* spring from different and independent manuscripts, the editor's usual tool in determining priority and authority, verbal collation, will not tell us which of these two manuscripts represents Sidney's final version. In the absence of compelling bibliographical evidence, the circumstances surrounding the publication of the *Defense* suggest that the Ponsonby text represents the manuscript Sidney last corrected.

William Ponsonby, publisher of the *Defense*, also published the "authorized" edition of Sidney's works for his sister, the Countess of Pembroke, as well as the sumptuous *Faery Queen* written by Sidney's friend, Spenser. Ponsonby entered "A treatise in commendation of Poetry or the Defence of Poesie . . . written by Sir Phillip Sidney" in the *Stationers' Register* on November 29, 1594.

Henry Olney is an evanescent figure in Elizabethan publishing. He may be the Henry Ovie, son of John Ovie, who was apprenticed to John Harrison in April, 1584. He was a bookseller in London in 1595 and 1596, selling books from his shop at the George near Cheap Gate in St. Paul's and then from his shop near Temple Gate. He published the *Apology* and Richard Lynche's *Diella*. He then disappears from extant records. Olney entered "a booke entituled an Apologie for Poetrie," without giving an author's name, on April 12, 1595. Olney's entry has been crossed out and underneath it another hand has written, "This belongeth to master ponsonby by a former

39. M. R. Mahl, "Introduction," in Sir Philip Sidney, *The Apology for Poetry* (Northridge: San Fernando Valley State College, 1969), pp. xix–xxi.

entrance and agreement is made between them whereby Master Ponsonby is to enjoy the copie according to the former entry."

Both the *Defense* and the *Apology* came out in 1595, and both show signs of hasty typesetting, proofreading and punctuation. W. H. Bond[40] argues that Ponsonby, acting in the capacity of Sidney's semi-official publisher, entered the *Defense*. Olney then entered the *Apology* without specifying an author in order to avoid a conflict with Ponsonby's claim to the copy through prior entrance. (Judging from his prefatory material, Olney, or his backer, felt that the *Defense* might not be published.) Olney published his *Apology* which, judging from the number of extant copies, sold well. Ponsonby cited his prior claim to the work and got possession of Olney's unbound sheets. He bound Olney's sheets with his own title page, canceling Olney's prefatory material, and sold the resulting book while hurriedly setting the *Defense* from his own manuscript, which he then issued as the "official" version.

Ponsonby reprinted the *Defense* in his 1598 folio edition of *The Countess of Pembrokes Arcadia . . . with sundry new additions*. He used the text of his *Defense* as copy-text for the folio, making some obvious corrections in grammar, spelling, and reference. He did not correct systematically, and he did not use Olney's *Apology* as a copy-text or as a major source of corrections. Since the 1598 folio was supervised, to some extent at least, by Sidney's sister, the *Defense* apparently seemed to her to be the most accurate version of what Sidney finally wrote. Certainly Ponsonby might have used the *Apology* had he wished, since he had legal possession of it.

The sequence of events I have just outlined indicates that, if either the Olney or the Ponsonby texts could be said to represent the manuscript last corrected by Sidney, the opinion of the semi-official publisher of his works and the opinion of his sister both incline to the *Defense* rather than the *Apology*. The circumstances of publication suggest that the truth resides in Ponsonby. The circumstances surrounding both entry and publication suggest that there may have been some question as to whether to publish or not (probably on the grounds that Sidney never finally finished it) and that Olney's publication of the *Apology* may have impelled the

40. Bond, "Bibliographical Jungle."

Countess of Pembroke and Ponsonby to proceed with the publication
of the *Defense*.

The circumstances surrounding the manuscript material available
to us seem to support these suppositions. Sidney allowed manuscripts of his works to circulate among his friends, but did not make
a practice of publishing them. Sir John Harington, a cousin of the
Sidney family, had read a manuscript version of the *Apology* before
1591, for, in his preface to his translation of Ariosto's *Orlando
Furioso* (1591), he refers to Sidney's work as an "apology" for
poetry. William Temple wrote a ramistical analysis of the "apology"
version in 1584. Since Sidney allowed his works to circulate in
manuscript and revised them while manuscript versions were
circulating, and since the Temple analysis establishes the existence
of a version of the *Apology* in 1584, I suspect that the *Apology* is the
version which Sidney allowed to circulate among his friends while
he revised it, in a desultory way, into the *Defense*.

The differences between the texts of the *Apology* and the *Defense*
seem to support this conjecture. The *Defense* shows signs of tidying
up. It uses Greek letters rather than Roman letters for Greek words.
On the whole, however, both versions are useful, and neither is to be
despised: Ponsonby contains some material that Olney does not;
Olney contains, for example, an explanatory phrase that Ponsonby
does not, and a correct reference which in Ponsonby is clearly
mistaken.

In editing the text for this edition, I have considered ease of
reading and semantic fullness as primarily important. This edition
purports only to present a semantically accurate and readable text
in modernized spelling based on what I consider to be Sidney's final
version of his work, the *Defense*.

In collating, I found that while the textual problem presented by
the variations between Ponsonby and Olney is nearly insoluble, the
semantic problem is relatively simple and straightforward and can be
solved by judicious conflation. Though it is important to a textual
analyst that Ponsonby reads "rhetoritian" and Olney "rethoritian,"
a modernized text need only recognize that the graphemic variants
both represent "rhetorician." When in the phrase "how *praxis* can be
without being moved to practice," Olney uses "cannot" for

Ponsonby's "can," the modernized text escapes the quandary which confronts the textual analyst: semantically, the two versions are equivalent, for Olney requires that "how" be read as meaning "that." When Ponsonby reads "St. Paul," and Olney reads "St. James," the editor of a modernized text need only refer to the Bible to discover that Sidney, quoting from memory as was his custom, had mistaken "Paul" for "James" and can accept the Olney reading. When Ponsonby reads "St. Paul himself sets a watchword upon philosophy," and Olney adds "Who yet for the credit of poets alleges twice two poets, and one of them by the name of a prophet," it is clear that in the interest of semantic fulness a modernized text should recognize the Olney supplement. All of the semantic problems connected with the text are of the orders which I have just noted.

Since Sidney apparently handled the *Defense* text last, I have based my text on Ponsonby's quarto, accepting silently corrections found in his folio. Since Sidney probably had not finished the *Defense*, and since variations in the Olney sometimes clarify his meaning, or expand it, I have accepted some Olney readings; I include the Ponsonby reading in the footnotes. I have silently modernized Sidney's spelling, and occasionally modernized or corrected obvious spelling and case and tense irregularities, but I have not attempted to modernize his vocabulary or his syntax, since I believe that the modern student can accustom himself, with moderate attention, to Sidney's use of the subjunctive and to his vocally oriented sentence structure.

Sidney himself apparently punctuated his text as though for vocal delivery. His typesetters punctuated almost *ad libitum*. I have silently simplified the punctuation, and regularized or modernized some of Sidney's habits, such as, for example, punctuating the end but not the beginning of a substantive member. With a few exceptions, I have not added any punctuation which is not warranted by some kind of punctuation in one or another of the texts. I have, however, silently dropped a great many punctuation marks. I have tried to retain the vocal orientation of the text, and generally use punctuation to represent rhetorical rather than grammatical members of the sentence, insofar as this punctuation will accord with modern reading habits. Ponsonby does not paragraph at all; Olney paragraphs in accordance with a principle which I make no pretense at understanding. I have paragraphed the *Defense*, consequently, as closely in accord with modern convention as I can without doing great violence to Sidney's rhetorically conceived transitions.

I translate Sidney's Latin and Greek phrases and quotations in the text unless Sidney himself provides a translation. In the notes at the foot of the page I include the original Latin and Greek, as well as any paraphrases which I felt were necessary to make reading easier, and identifications of those allusions, names, and quotations which the student might not readily recognize. In the supplementary notes at the back of the book I include references to possible sources and analogues, material illustrating the implications of Sidney's arguments, and references to recent scholarship which illuminates Sidney's meaning.

I introduced the rhetorical divisions into the text following K. O. Myrick's analysis of the rhetorical art of the *Defense*.[41]

LEWIS SOENS

University of Notre Dame

41. Myrick, *Sidney*.

THE DEFENSE OF POESY

The Defense of Poesy

When the right virtuous Edward Wotton[1] and I were at the Emperor's court together, we gave ourselves to learn horsemanship of John Pietro Pugliano, one that with great commendation had the place of an esquire in his stable, and he, according to the fertileness of the Italian wit, did not only afford us the demonstration of his practice, but sought to enrich our minds with the contemplations therein which he thought most precious. But with none I remember mine ears were at any time more loaded than when (either angered with slow payment or moved with our learner-like admiration) he exercised his speech in the praise of his faculty. He said soldiers were the noblest estate of mankind, and horsemen the noblest of soldiers. He said they were the masters of war and ornaments of peace, speedy goers and strong abiders, triumphers both in camps and courts. Nay, to so unbelieved[2] a point he proceeded, as that no earthly thing bred such wonder to a prince as to be a good horseman. Skill of government was but a pedantry in comparison. Then would he add certain praises by telling what a peerless beast the horse was, the only serviceable courtier without flattery, the beast of most beauty, faithfulness, courage, and such more that if I had not been a piece of a logician before I came to him, I think he would have persuaded me to have wished myself a horse.

But thus much at least, with his no few words, he drove into me, that self-love is better than any gilding to make that seem gorgeous wherein ourselves be parties. Wherein if Pugliano's strong affection and weak arguments will not satisfy you, I will give you a nearer

1. E.W.] *P;* Edward Wotton (1548–1626), half brother of Henry Wotton, Donne's friend. Wotton accompanied Sidney on a mission to the court of the Emperor Maximilian at Vienna in 1574–1575.
2. Unbelieved: unbelievable.

example of myself, who (I know not by what mischance) in these my not old years and idlest times having slipped into the title of a poet, am provoked to say something unto you in the defense of that my unelected vocation, which if I handle with more good will than good reasons, bear with me, since the scholar is to be pardoned that follows the steps of his master.

[*Narratio*]

And yet I must say that, as I have more just cause[3] to make a pitiful defense of poor poetry (which from almost the highest estimation of learning is fallen to be the laughingstock of children), so have I need to bring some more available[4] proofs, since the former[5] is by no man barred of his deserved credit. The silly latter has had even the names of philosophers used to the defacing of it, with great danger of civil war among the muses.

And first, truly, to all them that, professing learning, inveigh against poetry, may justly be objected that they go very near to ungratefulness to seek to deface that which (in the noblest nations and languages that are known) has been the first light-giver to ignorance and first nurse whose milk by[6] little and little enabled them to feed afterwards of tougher knowledges. And will they now[7] play the hedgehog that being received into the den, drove out his host? Or rather the vipers that with their birth kill their parents? Let learned Greece in any of his manifold sciences be able to show me one book before Musaeus, Homer, and Hesiod[8] (all three nothing else but poets). Nay, let any history be brought that can say any writers were there before them, if they were not men of the

3. More just cause: i.e., than Pugilano.
4. Available: availing.
5. The former: i.e., horsemanship.
6. by] *O; omit P.*
7. they now] *O;* you *P.*
8. Musaeus, according to legend, was the pupil of Orpheus. Hesiod (8th century B.C.), in his *Theogony*, writes of the gods; in *Works and Days*, he gives lessons in piety, myth, and agriculture. The poets in this list were commonly regarded as the "first theologians."

same skill (as Orpheus, Linus,[9] and some others are named) who, having been the first of that country that made pens deliverers of their knowledge to their[10] posterity, may[11] justly challenge to be called their fathers in learning.

For not only in time they had this priority (although in itself antiquity be venerable) but went before them as causes to draw with their charming sweetness the wild untamed wits to an admiration of knowledge. So as Amphion was said to move stones with his poetry to build Thebes, and Orpheus to be listened to by beasts (indeed stony and beastly people); so among the Romans were Livius Andronicus and Ennius;[12] so in the Italian language, the first that made it aspire to be a treasure-house of science were the poets Dante, Boccaccio, and Petrarch; so in our English were Gower and Chaucer, after whom, encouraged and delighted with their excellent fore-going, others have followed to beautify our mother tongue, as well in the same kind as in[13] other arts.

This did so notably show itself that the philosophers of Greece durst not a long time appear to the world but under the masks of poets. So Thales, Empedocles, and Parmenides sang their natural philosophy in verses. So did Pythagoras and Phocylides their moral counsels. So did Tyrtaeus in war matters[14] and Solon in matters of

9. Orpheus was a legendary magician, prophet, and poet; he was a son of the muse and a teacher of the Dionysiac mysteries. Linus was a legendary poet, supposedly the teacher of Orpheus.

10. their] *O;* the *P.*

11. may] *O;* nay *P.*

12. Amphion, according to legend, invented music and built the walls of Thebes with it; the legend was an allegory in the Renaissance for the capacity of music and poetry to civilize and harmonize. Livius Andronicus (284?–?204 B.C.) according to tradition, was the first to write poetry in Latin. Ennius (239?–?169 B.C.) was traditionally the greatest of the early Latin poets, the friend of Scipio, and civilizer of his era.

13. in] *O;* omit *P.*

14. Thales (640?–546 B.C.) traditionally wrote *Nautical Astronomy* and *On First Causes,* works of natural philosophy or "science"; Empedocles (490?–?430 B.C.) wrote the philosophical poems *On Nature* and *Purifications;* Parmenides (5th century B.C.) was an Eleatic moral philosopher who put his works into verse. Pythagoras (582?–?507 B.C.) was traditionally associated with Orphic poetry, and like the Orphic poets is said to have revealed his philosophy fully only to initiates; Phocylides (6th century B.C.) was traditionally a moral and proverbial

policy. Or rather, they, being poets, did exercise their delightful vein in those points of highest knowledge which before them lay hidden to the world. For that wise Solon was directly a poet, it is manifest, having written in verse the notable fable of the Atlantic island which was continued by Plato.

And truly, even Plato, whosoever well considers shall find that in the body of his work, though the inside and strength were philosophy, the skin as it were and beauty depended most of poetry, for all stands upon dialogues (wherein he feigns many honest burgesses of Athens to [15] speak of such matters that, if they had been set on the rack, they would never have confessed them), besides his poetical describing the circumstances of their meetings (as the well ordering of a banquet, the delicacy of a walk) with interlacing mere tales (as Gyge's ring and others) which who knows not to be flowers of poetry did never walk into Apollo's garden.

And even historiographers (although their lips sound of things done and verity be written in their foreheads) have been glad to borrow both fashion and perchance weight of the Poets. So Herodotus entitled his history by the name of the nine Muses, and both he and all the rest that followed him either stole or usurped of poetry their passionate describing of passions, the many particularities of battles (which no man could affirm) or, if that be denied me, long orations put in the mouths of great kings and captains (which it is certain they never pronounced).

So that truly neither philosopher nor historiographer could at the first have entered into the gates of popular judgments if they had not taken a great passport of poetry, which in all nations at this day where learning flourishes not is plain to be seen, in all which they have some feeling of poetry. In Turkey, besides their lawgiving divines, they have no other writers but poets. In our neighbor country Ireland, where truly learning goes very bare, yet are their poets held in a devout reverence. Even among the most barbarous and simple Indians, where no writing is, yet have they their poets who make and sing songs (which they call Areytos) [16] both of their

---

poet. Tyrtaeus (7th century B.C.): traditionally his poetry inspired the Spartans to fight and win.

15. to] *O; omit P.*

16. Areytos] *O;* Arentos *P.*

ancestors' deeds and praises of their gods—a sufficient probability
that if ever learning come among them, it must be by having their
hard dull wits softened and sharpened with the sweet delights of
poetry, for until they find a pleasure in the exercise of the mind,
great promises of much knowledge will little persuade them that
know not the fruits of knowledge. In Wales, the true remnant of the
ancient Britons, as there are good authorities to show the long time
they had poets (which they called bards), so through all the con-
quests of Romans, Saxons, Danes, and Normans (some of whom did
seek to ruin all memory of learning from among them) yet do their
poets even to this day last. So as it is not more notable in the soon
beginning than in long continuing.

But since the authors of most of our sciences were the Romans and
before them the Greeks, let us a little stand upon their authorities
but even so far as to see what names they have given unto this now
scorned skill. Among the Romans a poet was called *vates*, which is
as much as a "diviner," "foreseer," or "prophet," as by his con-
joined words *vaticinium* and *vaticinari* is manifest. So heavenly a title
did that excellent people bestow upon this heart-ravishing knowledge. And so far were they carried into the admiration thereof that
they thought in the chanceable hitting upon any of such verses,
great fore-tokens of their following fortunes were placed. Whereupon
grew the word of Virgilian lots,[17] when by sudden opening Virgil's
book they lighted upon some verse of his (as it is reported by many),
whereof the histories of the Emperors' lives are full (as of Albinus,
the governor of our island, who in his childhood met with this
verse, "I sieze arms madly, nor is there reason in arming,"[18] and
in his age performed it). Which[19] although it were a very vain and
godless superstition (as also it was to think spirits were commanded
by such verses, whereupon this word "charms," derived of *carmina*,
comes), so yet serves it to show the great reverence those wits were
held in. And altogether not without ground, since both[20] the oracles
of Delphos and Sibylla's prophecies were wholly delivered in verses,
for that same exquisite observing of number and measure in the

17. Virgilian lots: *Sortes Virgilianae.*
18. *Arma amens capio, nec sat rationis in armis* (*Aeneid*, II, 314).
19. Which] *O; omit P.*
20. both] by *P; omit O.*

words and that high-flying liberty of conceit proper to the poet did seem to have some divine force in it.

And may not I presume a little further to show the reasonableness of this word *vates* and say that the holy David's Psalms are a divine poem? If I do, I shall not do it without the testimony of great learned men, both ancient and modern. But even the name of "Psalms" will speak for me, which being interpreted is nothing but "songs"; then that it is fully written in meter, as all learned Hebricians agree, although the rules be not yet fully found; lastly and principally, his handling his prophecy, which is merely poetical. For what else is the awaking his musical instruments, the often and free changing of persons, his notable prosopopoeias (when he makes you, as it were, see God coming in His majesty, his telling of the beasts' joyfulness and hills' leaping) but a heavenly poesy, wherein almost he shows himself a passionate lover of that unspeakable and everlasting beauty to be seen by the eyes of the mind only cleared by faith? But truly now having named him, I fear I seem to profane that holy name, applying it to poetry which is among us thrown down to so ridiculous an estimation. But they that with quiet judgments will look a little deeper into it, shall find the end and working of it such as, being rightly applied, deserves not to be scourged out of the church of God.

But now let us see how the Greeks have named it, and how they deemed of it. The Greeks named him "Poet"[21] which name has, as the most excellent, gone through other languages. It comes of this word *poiein*,[22] which is "to make," wherein (I know not whether by luck or wisdom) we Englishmen have met with the Greeks in calling him a maker. Which name, how high and incomparable a title it is, I had rather were known by marking the scope of other sciences, than by my[23] partial allegation.

There is no art delivered unto mankind that has not the works of nature for his principal object, without which they could not consist and on which they so depend, as they become actors and players, as it were, of what nature will have set forth. So does the astronomer

21. Poet: ποιητής.
22. *Poiein:* ποιεῖν.
23. my] *O;* any *P.*

his very description (which no man will deny) shall not justly be barred from a principal commendation.

Poesy therefore is an art of imitation, for so Aristotle terms it in the word *mimesis*,[30] that is to say a representing, counterfeiting, or figuring forth (to speak metaphorically, a speaking picture) with this end, to teach and delight.

[*Partitio*]

Of this have been three general kinds. The chief both in antiquity and excellence were they that did imitate the inconceivable excellences of God. Such were David in his Psalms, Solomon in his Song of Songs, in his Ecclesiastes and Proverbs, Moses and Deborah in their hymns, and the writer of Job, which, beside other, the learned Emmanuel Tremellius and Franciscus[31] Junius do entitle the poetical part of the Scripture. Against these none will speak that has the Holy Ghost in due holy reverence. In this kind (though in a full wrong divinity) were Orpheus, Amphion, Homer in his *Hymns*, and many others, both Greeks and Romans. And this poesy must be used by whosoever will follow Saint James's[32] counsel in singing psalms when they are merry, and I know is used with the fruit of comfort by some when, in sorrowful pangs of their death-bringing sins, they find the consolation of the never-leaving goodness.

The second kind is of them that deal with matters philosophical: either moral (as Tyrtaeus, Phocylides, Cato) or natural (as Lucretius, and Virgil's *Georgics*) or astronomical (as Manilius and Pontanus) or historical (as Lucan),[33] which who mislike, the fault is in their judgment quite out of taste and not in the sweet food of

30. *Mimesis*: μίμσις.
31. Franciscus] *O;* F. *P.*
32. St. James's] *O* (St. James his); St. Paules *P.* From James 5:13 "Is any merry? Let him sing Psalms."
33. Dionysius Cato (4th century A.D.) traditionally wrote the *Disticha,* a collection of moral commonplaces popular in Renaissance schools. Manilius (1st century A.D.) wrote *Astronomica;* Giovanni Pontano (1426–1503) wrote *Urania,* a poem dealing with astronomy and the stars. Lucan (39–65 A.D.) wrote *Pharsalia,* a verse history of the Roman Civil wars.

sweetly uttered knowledge. But because this second sort is wrapped within the fold of the proposed subject and takes not the free course of his own invention, whether they properly be poets or no, let grammarians dispute and go to the third (indeed, right poets) of whom chiefly this question arises. Between whom and these second is such a kind of difference as between the meaner sort of painters, who counterfeit only such faces as are set before them, and the more excellent who, having no law but wit, bestow that in colors upon you which is fittest for the eye to see—as the constant, though lamenting, look of Lucretia when she punished in herself another's fault, wherein he paints not Lucretia (whom he never saw) but paints the outward beauty of such a virtue.

For these third be they which most properly do imitate to teach and delight, and to imitate, borrow nothing of what is, has been, or shall be, but range (only reined with learned discretion) into the divine consideration of what may be and should be. These be they that (as [34] the first and most noble sort) may justly be termed *vates*. So these are waited on in the excellentest languages and best understandings with the fore-described name of "poets." For these indeed do merely make to imitate, and imitate both to delight and teach, and delight to move men to take that goodness in hand which, without delight, they would fly as from a stranger, and teach to make them know that goodness whereunto they are moved (which, being the noblest scope to which ever any learning was directed, yet want there not idle tongues to bark at them).

These be subdivided into sundry more special denominations. The most notable be the heroic, lyric, tragic, comic, satiric, iambic, elegiac, pastoral, and certain others, some of these being termed according to the matter they deal with, some by the sort of verse they liked best to write in, for indeed the greatest part of poets have apparelled their poetical inventions in that numberous kind of writing which is called verse. Indeed, but appareled, verse being but an ornament and no cause to poetry, since there have been many most excellent poets that never versified and now swarm many versifiers that need never answer to the name of poets. For Xenophon who did imitate so excellently as to give us *effigiem justi imperii,*

34. As: like.

"the portraiture of a just empire," under the name of Cyrus (as Cicero says of him) [35] made therein an absolute heroical poem. So did Heliodorus in his sugared invention of that picture of love in Theagenes and Chariclea and yet both these wrote in prose, which I speak to show that it is not rhyming and versing that makes a poet (no more than a long gown makes an advocate, who, though he pleaded in armor, should be an advocate and no soldier), but it is that feigning notable images of virtues, vices, or what else, with that delightful teaching which must be the right describing note to know a poet by. Although indeed the senate of poets has chosen verse as their fittest rainment, meaning, as in matter they passed all in all, so in manner to go beyond them, not speaking (table-talk fashion, or like men in a dream) words as they chanceably fall from the mouth, but peizing [36] each syllable of each word by just proportion, according to the dignity of the subject.

[Confirmatio]

Now therefore it shall not be amiss first to weigh this latter sort of poetry by his works and then by his parts, and if in neither of these anatomies he be condemnable, I hope we shall obtain a more favorable sentence.

This purifying of wit, this enriching of memory, enabling of judgment, and enlarging of conceit, [37] which commonly we call learning, under what name soever it come forth, or to what immediate end soever it be directed, the final end is to lead and draw us to as high a perfection as our degenerate souls, made worse by their clay lodgings, can be capable of. This, according to the inclination of man, bred many-formed impressions. For some, that thought this felicity principally to be gotten by knowledge and no knowledge to be so high or heavenly as acquaintance with the stars, gave themselves to astronomy. Others, persuading themselves to be demigods if they knew the causes of things, became natural and supernatural philosophers. Some an admirable delight drew to music and some the certainty of demonstration to the mathematics, but all, one and

35. Cicero, *Epistles to Quintus*, I, i, viii, 23.
36. Peizing: weighing, measuring.
37. Conceit: imagination.

other, having this scope, to know and by knowledge to lift up the mind from the dungeon of the body to the enjoying his own divine essence.

But when by the balance of experience it was found that the astronomer looking to the stars might fall in a ditch, that the inquiring philosopher might be blind in himself and the mathematician might draw forth a straight line with a crooked heart, then, lo! did proof, the overruler of opinions, make manifest that all these are but serving sciences which, as they have each[38] a private end in themselves, so yet are they all directed to the highest end of the mistress-knowledge (by the Greeks called[39] architectonic[40]) which stands as I think in the knowledge of a man's self in the ethic and politic consideration, with the end of well-doing, and not of well-knowing only (even as the saddler's next end is to make a good saddle, but his further end to serve a nobler faculty, which is horsemanship; so the horseman's to soldiery, and the soldier not only to have the skill but to perform the practice of a soldier). So that the ending end of all earthly learning being virtuous action, those skills that most serve to bring forth that have a most just title to be princes over all the rest. Wherein, if we can show, the poet is worthy to have it[41] before any other competitors.

Among whom principally to challenge it step forth the moral philosophers, whom me thinks I see coming towards me with a sullen gravity as though they could not abide vice by daylight, rudely clothed for to witness outwardly their contempt of outward things, with books in their hands against glory whereto they set their names, sophistically speaking against subtlety and angry with any man in whom they see the foul fault of anger. These men (casting largess as they go of definitions, divisions, and distinctions) with a scornful interrogative do soberly ask whether it be possible to find any path so ready to lead a man to virtue as that which teaches what virtue is, and teaches it not only by delivering forth his very

38. each] *O; omit P.*
39. called] *O; omit P.*
40. *Architectonike*] *O;* ἀρχιτεκτονικη *P.*
41. It: i.e., the title of prince.

being, his causes and effects, but also by making known his enemy,
vice, which must be destroyed, and his cumbersome servant,
passion, which must be mastered; by showing the generalities that
contain it and the specialities that are derived from it; lastly, by
plain setting down, how it extends itself out of the limits of a man's
own little world to the government of families and maintaining of
public societies.

The historian scarcely gives leisure to the moralist to say so much
but that he, loaded with old mouse-eaten records, authorizing himself, for the most part, upon other histories (whose greatest authorities are built upon the notable foundation, hearsay), having much
ado to accord differing writers and to pick truth out of partiality,
better acquainted with a thousand years ago than with the present
age and yet better knowing how this world goes than how his own
wit runs, curious for antiquities and inquisitive of novelties, a wonder
to young folks and a tyrant in table-talk, denies in a great chafe that
any man for teaching of virtue and virtuous actions is comparable
to him. "I am the witness of time, the light of truth, the life of
memory, the governess of life, the herald of antiquity.[42] The
philosopher," says he, "teaches a disputative virtue, but I do an
active. His virtue is excellent in the dangerless Academy of Plato,
but mine shows forth her honorable face in the battles of Marathon,
Pharsalia, Poitiers, and Agincourt. He teaches virtue by certain
abstract considerations but I only bid you follow the footing of them
that have gone before you. Old-aged experience goes beyond the
fine-witted philosopher but I give the experience of many ages.
Lastly, if he make the song-book, I put the learner's hand to the
lute, and if he be the guide, I am the light." Then would he allege
you innumerable examples, confirming story by stories, how much
the wisest senators and princes have been directed by the credit of
history, as Brutus, Alphonsus of Aragon[43] (and who not, if need
be?). At length, the long line of their disputation makes a point in
this, that the one gives the precept and the other the example.

42. I am ... antiquity: *Testis temporum, lux veritatis, vita memoriae, magistra vitae,
nuntia vetustatis* (Cicero, *De Oratore*, II, ix, 36).
43. Alphonsus of Aragon (1416–1458): a patron of arts and learning.

Now whom shall we find (since the question stands for the highest form in the school of learning) to be moderator? Truly, as me seems, the poet. And if not a moderator, even the man that ought to carry the title from them both and much more from all other serving sciences. Therefore, compare we the poet with the historian and with the moral philosopher, and if he go beyond them both, no other human skill can match him. For as for the divine, with all reverence it is ever to be excepted, not only for having his scope as far beyond any of these as eternity exceeds a moment, but even for passing each of these in themselves. And for the lawyer, though *Jus* be the daughter of Justice, the chief of virtues, yet because he seeks to make men good rather through fear of punishment than through love of virtue,[44] or, to say righter, does not endeavor to make men good, but that their evil hurt not others, having no care, so he be a good citizen, how bad a man he be, therefore (as our wickedness makes him necessary and necessity makes him honorable) so is he not in the deepest truth to stand in rank with these who all endeavour to take naughtiness away and plant goodness even in the secretest cabinet of our souls. And these four are all that any way deal in the consideration of mens' manners, which being the supreme knowledge, they that best breed it deserve the best commendation.

The philosopher, therefore, and the historian are they which would win the goal; the one by precept, the other by example, but both, not having both, do both halt. For the philosopher, setting down with thorny arguments the bare rule, is so hard of utterance and so misty to be conceived that one that has no other guide but him shall wade in him till he be old before he shall find sufficient cause to be honest. For his knowledge stands so upon the abstract and general that happy is that man who may understand him and more happy that can apply what he does understand. On the other side, the historian, wanting the precept, is so tied, not to what should be, but to what is (to the particular truth of things and not to the general reason of things) that his example draws no necessary consequence and therefore a less fruitful doctrine.

44. Fear of punishment . . . love of virtue: *formidine poena . . . virtutis amore* (Horace, *Epistles* I, xvi, 52–53).

Now does the peerless poet perform both, for whatsoever the philosopher says should be done, he gives a perfect picture of it by someone by whom he presupposes it was done, so as[45] he couples the general notion with the particular example. A perfect picture, I say, for he yields to the powers of the mind an image of that whereof the philosopher bestows but a wordish description which does neither strike, pierce, nor possess the sight of the soul so much as that other does. For as in outward things, to a man that had never seen an elephant or a rhinoceros, who[46] should tell him most exquisitely all their shape, color, bigness and particular marks—or of a gorgeous palace the[47] architecture, who, declaring the full beauties, might well make the hearer able to repeat (as it were by rote) all he had heard—yet should never satisfy his inward conceit with being witness to itself of a true lively knowledge; but the same man, as soon as he might see those beasts well painted, or that house well in model, should straightways grow without need of any description to a judicial comprehending of them, so, no doubt, the philosopher with his learned definitions, be it of virtues or vices, matters of public policy or private government, replenishes the memory with many infallible grounds of wisdom which notwithstanding lie dark before the imaginative and judging power if they be not illuminated or figured forth by the speaking picture of poesy.

Tully takes much pains, and many times not without poetical helps, to make us know the force love of our country has in us. Let us but hear old Anchises speaking in the midst of Troy's flames, or see Ulysses in the fulness of all Calypso's delights bewail his absence from barren and beggarly Ithaca. Anger, the Stoics said, was a short madness.[48] Let but Sophocles bring you Ajax on a stage killing or whipping sheep and oxen, thinking them the army of Greeks with their chieftains Agamemnon and Menelaus, and tell me if you have not a more familiar insight into anger than finding in the schoolmen his genus and difference. See whether wisdom and temperance in Ulysses and Diomedes, valor in Achilles, friendship in Nisus and

---

45. so as: so that.
46. who: one who.
47. the] *O;* an *P.*
48. Seneca, *De Ira,* I, i, 2; Horace, *Epistles,* I, ii, 62.

Euryalus, even to an ignorant man, carry not an apparent shining, and contrarily, the remorse of conscience in Oedipus, the soon-repenting pride in Agamemnon, the self-devouring cruelty in his father Atreus, the violence of ambition in the two Theban brothers, the sour-sweetness of revenge in Medea, and (to fall lower) the Terentian Gnatho and our Chaucer's Pandar (so expressed that we now use their names to signify their trades), and finally, all virtues, vices, and passions so in their own natural states laid to the view that we seem not to hear of them but clearly to see through them.

But even in the most excellent determination of goodness, what philosopher's counsel can so readily direct a prince as the feigned Cyrus in Xenophon? Or a virtuous man in all fortunes as Aeneas in Virgil? Or a whole commonwealth, as the way of Sir Thomas More's *Utopia*? I say the way, because where Sir Thomas More erred, it was the fault of the man and not of the poet, for that way of patterning a commonwealth was most absolute, though he perchance has not so absolutely performed it. For the question is, whether the feigned image of poetry or the regular instruction of philosophy has the more force in teaching? Wherein if the philosophers have more rightly showed themselves philosophers than the poets have attained to the high top of their profession (as in truth "Neither gods, nor men, nor booksellers permit poets to be mediocre")[49] it is, I say again, not the fault of the art, but that by few men that art can be accomplished.

Certainly even our Saviour Christ could as well have given the moral commonplaces of uncharitableness and humbleness as the divine narration of Dives and Lazarus, or of disobedience and mercy as that heavenly discourse of the lost child and the gracious father, but that his through-searching wisdom knew the estate of Dives burning in hell and of Lazarus in Abraham's bosom would more constantly, as it were, inhabit both the memory and judgment (truly, for myself, me seems I see before my eyes the lost child's disdainful prodigality turned to envy a swine's dinner), which by the learned divines are thought not historical acts but instructing parables.

49. Neither . . . mediocre: *Mediocribus esse poetis/Non dii, non homines, non concessere columnae* (Horace, *Art of Poetry*, ll. 372–373 adapted).

For conclusion, I say the philosopher teaches, but he teaches obscurely, so as the learned only can understand him. That is to say, he teaches them that are already taught. But the poet is the food for the tenderest stomachs. The poet is indeed the right popular philosopher, whereof Aesop's tales give good proof, whose pretty allegories stealing under the formal tales of beasts make many, more beastly than beasts, begin to hear the sound of virtue from those dumb speakers.

But now may it be alleged that if this imagining of matters be so fit for the imagination, then must the historian needs surpass, who brings you images of true matters such as indeed were done and not such as fantastically or falsely may be suggested to have been done. Truly, Aristotle himself in his discourse of poesy plainly determines this question, saying that poetry is *philosophoteron* and *spoudaioteron*,[50] that is to say, it is more philosophical and more studiously serious[51] than history. His reason is, because poesy deals with *katholou*, that is to say with the universal consideration, and the history with *kath hekaston*,[52] the particular. Now, says he, the universal weighs what is fit to be said or done, either in likelihood or necessity (which the poesy considers in his imposed names) and the particular only marks whether Alcibiades did or suffered this or that. Thus far Aristotle, which reason of his, as all his, is most full of reason. For indeed if the question were whether it were better to have a particular act truly or falsely set down, there is no doubt which is to be chosen, no more than whether you had rather have Vespasian's[53] picture right as he was, or at the painter's pleasure, nothing resembling. But if the question be (for your own use and learning) whether it be better to have it set down as it should be or as it was, then certainly is more doctrineable[54] the feigned Cyrus in Xenophon than the true Cyrus in Justin, and the feigned Aeneas in Virgil than the right Aeneas in Dares Phrygius,[55] as, to a lady that desired to

50. *Philosophoteron*: φιλοσοφωτερον; *spoudaioteron*: σπουδαιότερον
51. studiously serious] *O;* omit *P.*
52. *Kathalou*: καθαλου; *Kath hekaston*: καθ ἑκαστον.
53. Vespasian (9–79 A.D.): Emperor (69–79 A.D.).
54. Doctrineable: meaningful.
55. Dares Phrygius (pre-Homeric): traditionally the author of a history of the Trojan war which actually dates ca. 5th century A.D.

fashion her countenance to the best grace, a painter should more benefit her to portrait a most sweet face, writing "Canidia" upon it, than to paint Canidia as she was, who, Horace swears, was full ill-favored.[56]

If the poet do his part aright, he will show you in Tantalus, Atreus,[57] and such like, nothing that is not to be shunned, in Cyrus, Aeneas, Ulysses, each thing to be followed, where the historian, bound to tell things as things were, cannot be liberal (without he will be poetical) of a perfect pattern but, as in Alexander or Scipio himself, show doings, some to be liked, some to be misliked, and then how will you discern what to follow but by your own discretion, which you had without reading Quintus Curtius?[58] And whereas a man may say, though in universal consideration of doctrine the poet prevails, yet that the history in his saying such a thing *was* done, does warrant a man more in that he shall follow, the answer is manifest that, if he stand upon that *was* (as if he should argue because it rained yesterday, therefore it should rain today), then indeed has it some advantage to a gross conceit. But if he know an example only informs a conjectured likelihood, and so go by reason, the poet does so far exceed him as he[59] is to frame his example to that which is most reasonable, be it in warlike, politic, or private matters, where the historian in his bare *was* has many times that which we call fortune to over-rule the best wisdom. Many times he must tell events whereof he can yield no cause, or if he do, it must be poetically.

For that a feigned example has as much force *to teach* as a true example (for as for *to move* it is clear, since the feigned may be tuned

56. Horace, *Epodes* V, and *Satires* I, viii, emphasizes the ugliness of the witch Canidia.

57. Tantalus and Atreus were both founders of the house of Pelops, and their sins laid the groundwork for later tragedies. Horace, *Art of Poetry*, l. 186 and *Satires*, I, i, 68, mentions them as examples of evil poetically useful. Renaissance critics allegorized Tantalus as the type of covetousness, from Horace, or as the type of the man who reveals the secrets of the gods, from Ovid.

58. Quintus Curtius (1st century A.D.): author of the *History* of Alexander. In spite of Sidney's implication of accuracy, his history is inaccurate. He emphasizes that power and conquest corrupted Alexander. Quintus] *O;* Q. *P.*

59. Him: the historian; he: his reader.

to the highest key of passion), let us take one example wherein an historian and a poet did concur. Herodotus and Justin[60] do both testify that Zopyrus, King Darius's faithful servant, seeing his master long resisted by the rebellious Babylonians, feigned himself in extreme disgrace of his king, for verifying of which he caused his own nose and ears to be cut off and so flying to the Babylonians was received and for his known valor so far credited that he did find means to deliver them over to Darius. Much-like matter does Livy[61] record of Tarquinius and his son. Xenophon excellently feigns such another stratagem, performed by Abradates in Cyrus's behalf.[62] Now would I fain know, if occasion be presented unto you to serve your prince by such an honest dissimulation, why you do not as well learn it of Xenophon's fiction as of the other's verity, and truly so much the better as you shall save your nose by the bargain, for Abradates did not counterfeit so far.

So then the best of the historian is subject to the poet, for whatsoever action or faction, whatsoever counsel, policy, or war-stratagem the historian is bound to recite, that may the poet, if he list, with his imitation make his own, beautifying it both for further teaching and more delighting as it please him, having all from Dante's heaven to his hell under the authority of his pen. Which if I be asked what poets have done so, as I might well name some, so yet say I, and say again, I speak of the art and not of the artificer.

Now to that which commonly is attributed to the praise of history in respect of the notable learning is got by marking the success, as though therein a man should see virtue exalted and vice punished, truly that commendation is peculiar to poetry and far off from history; for indeed poetry ever sets virtue so out in her best colors, making fortune her well-waiting handmaid, that one must needs be enamored of her. Well may you see Ulysses in a storm and in other hard plights, but they are but exercises of patience and magnanimity

60. Herodotus, *History*, III, 153–160; Justin, *Histories*, I, x. Arthur Golding, the puritan intellectual who completed Sidney's translation of Du Plessis de Mornay's *A Woorke Concerning the Trewenesse of the Christian Religion*, translated Justin into English in 1564.

61. Livy, *Histories*, I, liii–liv.

62. Xenophon, *Cyropaedia*, V–VII. The stratagem was practiced, not by Abradatas, but by Gadatas (V, iii, 8–19) and Araspas (VI, i, 39; iii, 14–19).

to make them shine the more in the near following prosperity. And of the contrary part, if evil men come to the stage, they ever go out (as the tragedy writer [63] answered to one that misliked the show of such persons) so manacled as they little animate folks to follow them. But the historian,[64] being captived to the truth of a foolish world, is many times a terror from well-doing and an encouragement to unbridled wickedness, for see we not valiant Miltiades rot in his fetters? the just Phocion and the accomplished Socrates put to death like traitors? the cruel Severus live prosperously? the excellent Severus miserably murdered? Sulla and Marius[65] dying in their beds? Pompey and Cicero slain then when they would have thought exile a happiness? See we not virtuous Cato driven to kill himself and rebel Caesar so advanced that his name yet after sixteen hundred years lasts in the highest honor?

And mark but even Caesar's own words of the forenamed Sulla (who in that only did honestly, to put down [66] his dishonest tryanny): "He knew no letters," as if want of learning caused him to do well. He meant it not by poetry which, not content with earthly plagues, devises new punishments in hell for tyrants, nor yet by philosophy which teaches "they must be killed,"[67] but no doubt by skill in

63. Euripides said of Ixion that he did not take him from the stage until he had bound him to a wheel, according to Plutarch, *Moralia*, I, ii, 19E.

64. historian] *O; Historie P.*

65. Miltiades (540?–?489 B.C.) saved his countrymen from the Persians by winning at Marathon and was imprisoned by those he saved; Cicero, *Republic*, I, iii, 5, is probably Sidney's authority. The Athenians condemned Phocion (402?–317 B.C.) to drink poison for his opposition to the popular party, according to Plutarch, *Life of Phocion*, 35–36. Septimius Severus (Emperor, A.D. 193–211) killed his rivals, Julianus, Pescennius Niger, and Clodius Albinus. Alexander Severus was Emperor, A.D. 222–235. Lucius Sulla (138–78 B.C.) was dictator for the senatorial party, fought Caius Marius, purged plebian party leaders, and voluntarily retired from the dictatorship; Caius Marius (155?–86 B.C.) led the plebian party against the Senate.

66. Put down: Suetonius (*Life of Caesar*, chap. lxxvii) says that Caesar said of Sulla, "Sullam nescisse literas, qui dictaturam deposuerit." Sidney, attributing "literas nescivit" to Caesar, ignores Caesar's pun (which depends upon the practice of the Roman school, wherein the teacher dictated to his little prisoners) but uses the Latin *deposuerit* when he says that Sulla "put down," that is "laid aside," his own dictatorship.

67. *Occidendos esse.*

history, for that indeed can afford you Cypselus,[68] Periander, Phalaris, Dionysius and I know not how many more of the same kennel that speed well enough in their abominable injustice of usurpation.

I conclude therefore that he excels history, not only in furnishing the mind with knowledge, but in setting it forward to that which deserves to be called and accounted good. Which setting forward and moving to well-doing indeed sets the laurel crown upon the poets as victorious, not only of the historian, but over the philosopher, howsoever in teaching it may be questionable. For suppose it be granted (that which I suppose with great reason may be denied) that the philosopher, in respect of his methodical proceeding, teach more perfectly than the poet, yet do I think that no man is so much a lover of philosophers[69] as to compare the philosopher in moving with the poet. And that moving is of a higher degree than teaching, it may by this appear, that it is well nigh both the cause and effect of teaching, for who will be taught if he be not moved with desire to be taught? And what so much good does that teaching bring forth (I speak still of moral doctrine) as that it moves one to do that which it does teach? For as Aristotle says, it is not knowing, but doing must be the fruit[70]—and how doing can be without being moved to practice, it is no hard matter to consider.

The philosopher shows you the way. He informs you of the particularities, as well of the tediousness of the way as of the pleasant lodging you shall have when your journey is ended, as of the many by-turnings that may divert you from your way. But this is to no man but to him that will read him and read him with attentive, studious painfulness, which constant desire, whosoever has in him has already passed half the hardness of the way and therefore is beholding to the philosopher but for the other half. Nay truly, learned men have learnedly thought that where once reason has so

68. Cypselus was tyrant of Corinth (655?–625 B.C.). Periander was Cypselus's son. Phalaris was tyrant of Agrigento (570–554 B.C.) and Dionysius the Elder was tyrant of Syracuse (405–367 B.C.). Each of these tyrants died peacefully in his bed.

69. Lover of philosophers: φιλοφιλοσοφος; *philophilosophos;* lover of the lovers of wisdom.

70. *gnosis,* knowing, γνωσις; *praxis,* doing, πραξις (Aristotle, *Ethics,* I, iii, 1095a).

much over-mastered passion as that the mind has a free desire to do well, the inward light each mind has in itself is as good as a philosopher's book, since in nature we know it is well to do well and what is well and what is evil, although not in the words of art which philosophers bestow upon us (for out of natural conceit the philosophers drew it), but to be moved to do that which we know, or to be moved with desire to know, "this is the labor, this the toil." [71]

Now therein of all sciences (I speak still of human and according to the human conceit) is our poet the monarch, for he does not only show the way, but gives so sweet a prospect into the way as will entice any man to enter into it. Nay, he does as if your journey should lie through a fair vineyard, at the very first give you a cluster of grapes, that, full of that taste, you may long to pass further. He begins not with obscure definitions which must blur the margin with interpretations and load the memory with doubtfulness, but he comes to you with words set in delightful proportion, either accompanied with or prepared for the well-enchanting skill of music. And with a tale, forsooth, he comes unto you, with a tale which holds children from play and old men from the chimney corner, and, pretending no more, does intend the winning of the mind from wickedness to virtue, even as the child is often brought to take most wholesome things by hiding them in such other as have a pleasant taste, which, if one should begin to tell them the nature of the aloes or rhubarb they should receive, would sooner take their physic at their ears than at their mouth. So is it in men, most of which are childish in the best things till they be cradled in their graves. Glad they will be to hear the tales of Hercules, Achilles, Cyrus, Aeneas, and hearing them, must needs hear the right description of wisdom, valor, and justice, which, if they had been barely (that is to say, philosophically) set out, they would swear they be brought to school again.

That imitation whereof poetry is has the most conveniency to nature of all other, insomuch that (as Aristotle says)[72] those things which in themselves are horrible, as cruel battles, unnatural monsters, are made in poetical imitation delightful. Truly, I have

71. *Hoc opus, hic labor est* (Virgil, *Aeneid*, VI, 129).
72. Aristotle, *Poetics*, IV, 1448b.

known men that even with reading *Amadis de Gaulle*[73] (which God knows wants much of a perfect poesy) have found their hearts moved to the exercise of courtesy, liberality and especially courage. Who reads Aeneas carrying old Anchises on his back that wishes not it were his fortune to perform so excellent an act? Whom do[74] not those words of Turnus move (the tale of Turnus having planted his image in the imagination), "Shall this land see him fleeing? In such a plight is death, then, so miserable?"[75] Where the philosophers, as they think, scorn to delight, so must they be content little to move (saving wrangling whether virtue be the chief or the only good, whether the contemplative or the active life do excel) which Plato and Boethius[76] well knew and therefore made mistress Philosophy very often borrow the masking rainment of poesy. For even those hard-hearted evil men who think virtue a school-name and know no other good but "please yourself,"[77] and therefore despise the austere admonitions of the philosopher and feel not the inward reason they stand upon, yet will be content to be delighted (which is all the good fellow poet seems to promise) and so steal to see the form of goodness (which seen, they cannot but love) ere themselves be aware, as if they took a medicine of cherries.

Infinite proofs of the strange effects of this poetical invention might be alleged. Only two shall serve, which are so often remembered as, I think, all men know them. The one of Menenius Agrippa, who, when the whole people of Rome had resolutely divided themselves from the senate with apparent show of utter ruin, though he were for that time an excellent orator, came not among them upon trust either of figurative speeches or cunning insinuations, and much less with far-fetched maxims of philosophy which (especially if they were Platonic) they must have learned geometry before they could

73. A chivalric romance by Vasco de Lobeira which Sidney used as a source for his *Arcadia.*

74. do] *O ;* does *P.*

75. *Fugientem haec terra videbit? Usqueadeone mori miserum est?* (Virgil, *Aeneid,* XII, 645–646). Turnus is the Latian hero whom Aeneas finally defeats.

76. Boethius (A.D. 480?–?524) wrote the menippean *satura,* the *Consolation of Philosophy* (A.D. ?524), in which prose and verse alternate and Philosophy is a major character.

77. *Indulgere genio,* from *indulge genio* (Persius, *Satires,* V, 151).

well have conceived, but forsooth, he behaves himself like a homely and familiar poet. He tells them a tale, that there was a time when all the parts of the body made a mutinous conspiracy against the belly, which they thought devoured the fruits of each other's labor. They concluded they would let so unprofitable a spender starve. In the end, to be short (for the tale is notorious and as notorious that it was a tale), with punishing the belly, they plagued themselves. This applied by him wrought such effect in the people as[78] I never read that only words brought forth but[79] then so sudden and so good an alteration, for upon reasonable conditions a perfect reconcilement ensued.

The other is of Nathan the prophet,[80] who when the holy David had so far forsaken God as to confirm adultery with murder, when he was to do the tenderest office of a friend in laying his own shame before his eyes, sent by God to call again so chosen a servant, how does he it but by telling of a man whose beloved lamb was ungratefully taken from his bosom (the application most divinely true, but the discourse itself feigned), which made David (I speak of the second and instrumental cause) as in a glass see his own filthiness, as that heavenly Psalm of mercy[81] well testifies.

By these, therefore, examples and reasons, I think it may be manifest that the poet, with that same hand of delight, does draw the mind more effectually than any other art does, and so a conclusion not unfitly ensues: that as virtue is the most excellent resting place for all worldly learning to make his end of, so poetry, being the most familiar to teach it, and most princely to move towards it, in the most excellent work, is the most excellent workman.

But I am content not only to decipher him by his works (although works, in commendation and dispraise, must ever hold a high authority) but more narrowly will examine his parts so that, as in man, though all together may carry a presence full of majesty and beauty, perchance in some one defectious piece we may find blemish.

78. As: that.
79. But: except.
80. 2 Samuel 12.
81. Psalms 51.

Now in his parts, kinds, or species (as you list to term them) it is to be noted that some poesies have coupled together two or three kinds (as the tragical and comical, whereupon is risen the tragicomical), some in the like[82] manner have mingled prose and verse (as Sannazaro[83] and Boethius), some have mingled matters heroical and pastoral, but that comes all to one in this question, for, if severed they be good, the conjunction cannot be hurtful. Therefore, perchance forgetting some and leaving some as needless to be remembered, it shall not be amiss in a word to cite the special kinds to see what faults may be found in the right use of them.

Is it then the pastoral poem which is misliked? (for perchance where the hedge is lowest, they will soonest leap over). Is the poor pipe disdained which sometimes out of Meliboeus's mouth can show the misery of people under hard lords and ravening soldiers, and again, by Tityrus,[84] what blessedness is derived to them that lie lowest from the goodness of them that sit highest; sometimes under the pretty tales of wolves and sheep can include the whole considerations of wrongdoing and patience; sometimes show that contentions for trifles can get but a trifling victory; where perchance a man may see that even Alexander and Darius, when they strove who should be cock of this world's dunghill, the benefit they got was that the after-livers may say, "These lines I learned to remember when beaten Thyrsis tried in vain to win. Since then Corydon, Corydon is the man of the hour."[85]

Or is it the lamenting elegiac, which in a kind heart would move rather pity than blame, who bewails with the great philosopher Heraclitus[86] the weakness of mankind and the wretchedness of the world, who surely is to be praised either for compassionate

82. like] O; omit P.

83. Jacopo Sannazaro (1458–1530) wrote widely esteemed *Eclogues* and the pastoral romance *Arcadia*, which Sidney used in his own *Arcadia*.

84. Meliboeus represents those Romans who were dispossessed of their land by Augustus after the civil wars; Tityrus represents those Romans to whom Augustus restored their lands (Virgil, *Eclogues*, I).

85. *Haec memini et victum frustra contendere Thyrsim. Ex illo Corydon, Corydon, est tempore nobis* (Virgil, *Eclogues*, VII, 69–70).

86. Heraclitus (6th–5th century B.C.) was known as the weeping philosopher (Juvenal, *Satires*, X, 30).

accompanying just causes of lamentations or for rightly painting out how weak be the passions of woefulness? Is it the bitter but wholesome iambic, who rubs the galled mind in making shame the trumpet of villainy with bold and open crying out against naughtiness? Or the satiric who, "the rascal, probes at every vice of his laughing friend,"[87] who sportingly never leaves till he make a man laugh at folly, and, at length ashamed, to laugh at himself, which he cannot avoid without avoiding the folly; who, while "he plays around the heart,"[88] gives us to feel how many headaches a passionate life brings us to, how, when all is done, "Ulubrae is as good as anywhere, if our calmness of mind doesn't fail us?"[89]

No? Perchance it is the comic, whom naughty play-makers and stage-keepers have justly made odious. To the arguments of abuse, I will after answer. Only thus much now is to be said, that the comedy is an imitation of the common errors of our life, which he represents in the most ridiculous and scornful sort that may be, so as it is impossible that any beholder can be content to be such a one. Now as in geometry the oblique must be known as well as the right, and in arithmetic the odd as well as the even, so in the actions of our life, who sees not the filthiness of evil wants a great foil to perceive the beauty of virtue. This does the comedy handle so in our private and domestical matters as, with hearing it, we get (as it were) an experience what is to be looked for of a niggardly Demea, of a crafty Davus, of a flattering Gnatho, of a vain-glorious Thraso,[90] and not only to know what effects are to be expected, but to know who be such by the signifying badge given them by the comedian. And little reason has any man to say that men learn the evil by seeing it so set out, since (as I said before) there is no man living, but by the force truth has in nature, no sooner sees these men play their parts, but wishes them at hard labor,[91] although perchance the

87. *Omne vafer vitium ridenti tangit amico* (Persius, *Satires* I, 116–117, adapted). Persius refers to Horace.

88. *Circum praecordia ludit* (Persius, *Satires*, I, 117).

89. *Est Ulubris, animus si nos non deficit aequus* (Horace, *Epistles*, I, xi, 30, adapted).

90. Demea is the miserly father in Terence's *Adelphi*. Davus is the sly servant in Terence's *Eunuch*. From Thraso, we get "thrasonical."

91. At hard labor: *in pistrinum* (Terence, *Andria*, I, ii, 27; Plautus, *Mostellaria*, I, i, 16). Slaves were sent to work in the mill as punishment.

sack of his own faults lie so behind his back that he sees not himself to dance the same measure, whereto yet nothing can more open his eyes than to see his own actions contemptibly set forth.

So that the right use of comedy will, I think, by nobody be blamed, and much less of the high and excellent tragedy, that opens the greatest wounds and shows forth the ulcers that are covered with tissue, that makes kings fear to be tyrants and tyrants manifest their tyrannical humors, that with stirring the affects of admiration and commiseration teaches the uncertainty of this world and upon how weak foundations gilden roofs are built, that makes us know "who wields a fell scepter in a harsh empire fears the frightened, terror returns on its author."[92] But how much it can move, Plutarch yields a notable testimony of the abominable tyrant Alexander Pheraeus, from whose eyes a tragedy well made and represented drew abundance of tears, who without all pity had murdered infinite numbers, and some of his own blood.[93] So as he, that was not ashamed to make matters for tragedies, yet could not resist the sweet violence of a tragedy, and if it wrought no further good in him, it was that he, in despite of himself, withdrew himself from hearkening to that which might mollify his hardened heart. But it is not the tragedy they do mislike, for it were too absurd to cast out so excellent a representation of whatsoever is most worthy to be learned.

Is it the lyric that most displeases, who with his tuned lyre and well-accorded voice gives praise, the reward of virtue, to virtuous acts, who gives moral precepts and natural problems, who sometimes raises up his voice to the height of the heavens in singing the lauds of the immortal God? Certainly (I must confess my own barbarousness) I never heard the old song of Percy and Douglas that I found not my heart moved more than with a trumpet, and yet is it sung but by some blind crowder with no rougher voice than rude style. Which being so evil appareled in the dust and cobwebs of that uncivil age, what would it work trimmed in the gorgeous eloquence of Pindar?[94] In Hungary I have seen it the manner at all

92. *Qui sceptra duro saevuus imperio regit, timet timentes, metus in auctorem redit* (Seneca, *Oedipus*, III, 705–706).
93. Plutarch tells this story in *Life of Pelopidas*, 29.
94. Pindar (522?–443 B.C.) was the most famous Greek lyric poet.

feasts and other such like meetings to have songs of their ancestors' valor, which that right soldier-like nation think one of the chiefest kindlers of brave courage. The incomparable Lacedaemonians did not only carry that kind of music ever with them to the field but even at home, as such songs were made, so were they all content to be singers of them, when the lusty men were to tell what they did, the old men what they had done, and the young what they would do.[95] And where a man may say that Pindar many times praises highly victories of small moment, rather matters of sport than virtue, as it may be answered it was the fault of the poet and not of the poetry, so indeed the chief fault was in the time and custom of the Greeks, who set those toys at so high a price that Philip of Macedon reckoned a horse race won at Olympus among his three fearful felicities.[96] But, as the inimitable Pindar often did, so is that kind most capable and most fit to awake the thoughts from the sleep of idleness to embrace honorable enterprises.

There rests the heroical, whose very name, I think, should daunt all backbiters. For by what conceit can a tongue be directed to speak evil of that which draws with him no less champions than Achilles, Cyrus, Aeneas, Turnus, Tydeus, Rinaldo;[97] who does not only teach and move to a truth, but teaches and moves to the most high and excellent truth; who makes magnanimity and justice shine through all misty fearfulness and foggy desires; who (if the saying of Plato and Tully be true, that who could see virtue would be wonderfully ravished with the love of her beauty)—this man sets her out to make her more lovely in her holiday apparel to the eye of any that will deign not to disdain until they understand. But if anything be already said in the defense of sweet poetry, all concurs to the maintaining the heroical, which is not only a kind, but the best and most accomplished kind, of poetry. For, as the image of each action

95. Plutarch describes this custom in *Life of Lycurgus*, 21.

96. Philip of Macedon (382–336 B.C.) was the father of Alexander. Plutarch tells this story in *Life of Alexander*, chap. 3. Sidney confuses Olympus with Olympias.

97. Tydeus (in Statius's *Thebaid*) and Rinaldo (in Ariosto's *Orlando* and Tasso's *Rinaldo* and *Gerusalemme Liberata*) are, like Achilles, Cyrus, Aeneas, and Turnus, epic heroes and moral exemplars.

stirs and instructs the mind, so the lofty image of such worthies
most inflames the mind with desire to be worthy, and informs with
counsel how to be worthy. Only let Aeneas be worn in the tablet
of your memory, how he governs himself in the ruin of his country
in the preserving his old father and carrying away his religious
ceremonies, in obeying god's commandment to leave Dido though
not only all passionate kindness but even the humane consideration
of virtuous gratefulness would have craved other of him, how in
storms, how in sports, how in war, how in peace, how a fugitive,
how victorious, how beseiged, how beseiging, how to strangers,
how to allies, how to enemies, how to his own, lastly, how in his
inward self and how in his outward government, and I think (in a
mind not [98] prejudiced with a prejudicating humor) he will be found
in excellency fruitful. Yea, as Horace says "better than Chrysippus
or Crantor." [99]

But truly I imagine it falls out with these poet-whippers as with
some good women, who often are sick but in faith they cannot tell
where, so the name of poetry is odious to them but neither his cause
nor effects, neither the sum that contains him nor the particularities
descending from him give any fast handle to their carping
dispraise.

Since, then, poetry is of all human learnings the most ancient and
of most fatherly antiquity (as from whence other learnings have
taken their beginnings); since it is so universal that no learned
nation does despise it nor barbarous nation is without it; since both
Roman and Greek gave such divine names unto it (the one of
prophesying, the other of making, and that indeed that name of
making is fit for him, considering that, where all other arts retain
themselves within their subject and receive, as it were, their being
from it, the poet only, only brings his own stuff and does not learn a
conceit out of a matter, but makes matter for a conceit); since
neither his description nor end containing any evil, the thing

98. not] *O;* moste *P.*

99. *Melius Chrysippo et Crantore* (Horace, *Epistles*, I, ii, 4). Chrysippus (280?–
?207 B.C.) was a stoic philosopher. Crantor (4th century B.C.) was a commentator
on Plato.

described cannot be evil; since his effects be so good as to teach goodness and delight the learners of it; since therein (namely in moral doctrine, the chief of all knowledges) he does not only far pass the historian but for instructing is well nigh comparable to the philosopher and [100] for moving leaves him behind him; since the Holy Scripture (wherein there is no uncleanness) has whole parts in it poetical, and that even our Savior Christ vouchsafed to use the flowers of it; since all his kinds are not only in their united forms but in their severed dissections fully commendable, I think (and think I think rightly) the laurel crown appointed for triumphant captains does worthily, of all other learnings, honor the poets' triumph.

[Reprehensio]

But because we have ears as well as tongues and that the lightest reasons that may be will seem to weigh greatly if nothing be put in the counterbalance, let us hear and (as well as we can) ponder what objections be made against this art which may be worthy either of yielding or answering.

First, truly, I note, not only in these *misomusoi*,[101] poet-haters, but in all that kind of people who seek a praise by dispraising others, that they do prodigally spend a great many wandering words in quips and scoffs, carping and taunting at each thing, which, by stirring the spleen, may stay the brain from a through-beholding the worthiness of the subject. Those kind of objections, as they are full of a very idle easiness (since there is nothing of so sacred a majesty but that an itching tongue may rub itself upon it), so deserve they no other answer but, instead of laughing at the jest, to laugh at the jester. We know a playing wit can praise the discretion of an ass, the comfortableness of being in debt, and the jolly commodities of being sick of the plague,[102] so, of the contrary side, if we will turn

100. and] *O; omit P.*

101. *Misomusoi:* μισομυσοι.

102. Cornelius Agrippa (1486?–1535) praises an ass in *The Incertitude and Vanity of the Sciences and Arts,* chap. 102. Francesco Berni (1497–1536) wrote orations in praise of debt and the plague.

Ovid's verse *"ut lateat virtus proximitate mali"* [103] (that good lie hid in nearness of the evil), Agrippa will be as merry in showing the vanity of science as Erasmus was in the commending of folly. Neither shall any man or matter escape some touch of these smiling railers. (But for Erasmus and Agrippa, they had another foundation than the superficial part would promise.) Marry, these other pleasant fault-finders, who will correct the verb before they understand the noun and confute others' knowledge before they confirm their own, I would have them only remember that scoffing comes not of wisdom, so as the best title in true English they get with their merriments is to be called good fools, for so have our grave forefathers ever termed that humorous kind of jesters.

But that which gives greatest scope to their scorning humor is rhyming and versing. It is already said (and, as I think, truly said), it is not rhyming and versing that makes poesy. One may be a poet without versing, and a versifier without poetry. But yet presuppose it were inseparable (as indeed it seems Scaliger judges), truly it were an inseparable commendation. For if *oratio* next to *ratio* [104] (speech next to reason) be the greatest gift bestowed upon mortality, that cannot be praiseless which does most polish that blessing of speech, which considers each word not only (as a man may say) by his forcible quality, but by his best-measured quantity (carrying even in themselves a harmony), without, perchance, number, measure, order, proportion be in our time grown odious.

But lay aside the just praise it has by being the only fit speech for music (music, I say, the most divine striker of the senses). Thus much is undoubtedly true, that if reading be foolish without remembering, memory being the only treasure [105] of knowledge, those words which are fittest for memory are likewise most convenient for knowledge. Now that verse far exceeds prose in the knitting up of the memory, the reason is manifest, the words (besides their delight, which has a great affinity to memory) being so set as one cannot be lost, but the whole work fails, which, accusing itself,

103. Ovid, *The Art of Love*, II, 661–662, adapted.
104. A commonplace. See Quintilian, *Institutes*, II, xvi; Cicero, *Offices*, I, 16, 50–51.
105. Treasure: treasury.

calls the remembrance back to itself and so most strongly confirms it. Besides, one word so (as it were) begetting another, as be it in rhyme or measured verse, by the former a man shall have a near guess to the follower. Lastly, even they that have taught the art of memory have showed nothing so apt for it as a certain room divided into many places, well and thoroughly known. Now that has the verse in effect perfectly, every word having his natural seat, which seat must needs make the word remembered. But what needs more in a thing so known to all men? Who is it that ever was scholar that does not carry away some verses of Virgil, Horace, or Cato which in his youth he learned and even to his old age serve him for hourly lessons; as "Shun a pryer, for he's also a gossip," "While each is out for himself, we are a pack of suckers." [106] But the fitness it has for memory is notably proved by all delivery of arts, wherein for the most part, from grammar to logic, mathematics, physic, and the rest, the rules chiefly necessary to be borne away are compiled in verses. So that verse being in itself sweet and orderly, and being best for memory (the only handle of knowledge) it must be in jest that any man can speak against it.

Now then go we to the most important imputations laid to the poor poets. For aught I can yet learn, they are these: first, that there being many other more fruitful knowledges, man might better spend his time in them than in this; secondly, that it is the mother of lies; thirdly, that it is the nurse of abuse, infecting us with many pestilent desires, with a siren's sweetness drawing the mind to the serpent's tail of sinful fancies (and herein especially comedies give the largest field to ear, [107] as Chaucer says); how both in other nations and in ours, before poets did soften us, we were full of courage, given to martial exercises, the pillars of manlike liberty and not lulled asleep in shady idleness with poets' pastimes; and lastly and chiefly, they cry out with open mouth (as if they had overshot Robin Hood) that Plato banished them out of his commonwealth. Truly this is much, if there be much truth in it.

First to the first. That a man might better spend his time is a

---

106. *Percontatorem fugito nam garrulus idem est* (Horace, *Epistles*, I, xviii, 69); *Dum tibi quisque placet, credula turba sumus* (Ovid, *Remedia Amoris*, l. 686, adapted).

107. Ear: from Old English *erian*, "plow." Chaucer, *Knight's Tale*, l. 28.

reason indeed, but it does, as they say, but beg the question.[108] For if it be, as I affirm, that no learning is so good as that which teaches and moves to virtue and that none can both teach and move thereto so much as poesy, then is the conclusion manifest that ink and paper cannot be to a more profitable purpose employed. And certainly, though a man should grant their first assumption, it should follow, methinks, very unwillingly that good is not good because better is better. But I still and utterly deny that there is sprung out of earth a more fruitful knowledge.

To the second, therefore, that they should be the principal liars, I answer paradoxically (but truly, I think truly) that of all writers under the sun, the poet is the least liar and, though he would, as a poet can scarcely be a liar. The astronomer, with his cousin the geometrician, can hardly escape when they take upon them to measure the height of the stars. How often, think you, do the physicians lie when they aver things good for sicknesses which afterwards send Charon a great number of souls drowned in a potion before they come to his ferry? And no less of the rest which take upon them to affirm. Now for the poet, he nothing affirms and therefore never lies, for, as I take it, to lie is to affirm that to be true which is false. So as the other artists, and especially the historian, affirming many things, can in the cloudy knowledge of mankind hardly escape from many lies.

But the poet, as I said before, never affirms. The poet never makes any circles about your imagination, to conjure you to believe for true what he writes. He cites not authorities of other histories, but even for his entry calls the sweet muses to inspire unto him a good invention, in troth, not laboring to tell you what is or is not, but what should or should not be. And therefore, though he recount things not true, yet because he tells them not for true, he lies not, without we will say that Nathan lied in his speech before alleged to David. Which as a wicked man durst scarce say, so think I none so simple would say[109] that Aesop lied in the tales of his beasts (for who

108. Beg the question: *petere principium*.
109. Without . . . would say: i.e., unless we will also grant that Nathan lied to David, and just as no man is wicked enough to dare to say that, so there is no man who is simple-minded enough to say . . . .

thinks that Aesop wrote it for actually true, were well worthy to have his name chronicled among the beasts he writes of). What child is there that, coming to a play and seeing "Thebes" written in great letters upon an old door, does believe that it is Thebes? If then a man can arrive to the child's age to know that the poets' persons and doings are but pictures what should be, and not stories what have been, they will never give the lie to things not affirmatively, but allegorically and figuratively written. And therefore as in history, looking for truth, they may go away full-fraught with falsehood, so in poesy, looking but for fiction, they shall use the narration but as an imaginative ground-plat of a profitable invention.

But hereto is replied that the poets give names to men they write of, which argues a conceit of an actual truth, and so, not being true, proves a falsehood. And does the lawyer lie then, when under the names of John-of-the-Stile, and John-of-the-Nokes, he puts his case? But that is easily answered. Their naming of men is but to make their picture the more lively and not to build any history. Painting men, they cannot leave men nameless. We see we cannot play at chess but that we must give names to our chessmen, and yet methinks he were a very partial champion of truth that would say we lied for giving a piece of wood the reverend title of a bishop. The poet names Cyrus and Aeneas no other way than to show what men of their fames, fortunes, and estates should do.

Their third is how much it abuses men's wit, training it to wanton sinfulness and lustful love. For indeed that is the principal, if not only, abuse I can hear alleged. They say the comedies rather teach than reprehend amorous conceits. They say the lyric is larded with passionate sonnets, the elegiac weeps the want of his mistress, and that even to the heroical, Cupid has ambitiously climbed. Alas, Love, I would you could as well defend yourself as you can offend others. I would those on whom you do attend could either put you away, or yield good reason why they keep you. But grant love of beauty to be a beastly fault (although it be very hard, since only man and no beast has that gift to discern beauty); grant that lovely name of Love to deserve all hateful reproaches (although even some of my masters the philosophers spent a good deal of their lamp-oil in setting forth the excellency of it); grant, I say, what they will have granted, that not only love, but lust, but vanity, but (if they list) scurrility possess many leaves of the poets' books, yet think I, when this is granted, they will find their sentence may with good manners put the last words foremost and not say that poetry abuses man's wit, but that man's wit abuses poetry. For I will not deny but that man's wit may make poetry, which should be *eikastike* (which some learned have defined "figuring forth good things") to be *phantastike*[110] (which does contariwise infect the fancy with unworthy objects); as the painter, that[111] should give to the eye either some excellent perspective or some fine picture, fit for building or fortification or containing in it some notable example (as Abraham sacrificing his son Isaac, Judith killing Holofernes, David fighting with Goliath), may leave those and please an ill-pleased eye with wanton shows of better-hidden matters. But what, shall the abuse of a thing make the right use odious? Nay, truly, though I yield that poesy may not only be abused but that being abused, by the reason of his sweet charming force, it can do more hurt than any other army of words, yet shall it be so far from concluding that the abuse should give reproach to the abused that, contrariwise, it is a good reason that whatsoever being abused does most harm, being rightly used (and upon the right use, each thing receives his title) does most good. Do we not see skill of physic, the best rampire[112] to our often-assaulted bodies, being abused, teach poison, the most violent destroyer? Does not knowledge of the law, whose end is to even and right all things, being abused, grow the crooked fosterer of horrible injuries? Does not (to go to the highest) God's word abused breed heresy and His Name abused become blasphemy? Truly, a needle cannot do much hurt, and as truly (with leave of ladies be it spoken) it cannot do much good. With a sword you may kill your father, and with a sword you may defend your prince and country. So that as in their calling poets fathers of lies, they said nothing, so in this, their argument of abuse, they prove the commendation.

They allege herewith that before poets began to be in price, our nation had set their hearts' delight upon action and not imagination,

---

110. *Eikastike:* εἰκαστικὴ; *phantastike:* φανταστικὴ.
111. that] *O;* omit *P.*
112. Rampire: rampart.

rather doing things worthy to be written than writing things fit to be done. What that before-time was, I think scarcely Sphinx can tell, since no memory is so ancient that has not the precedence of poetry.[113] And certain it is that in our plainest homeliness, yet never was the Albion nation without poetry.

Marry, this argument, though it be leveled against poetry, yet is it indeed a chain-shot against all learning, or bookishness (as they commonly term it). Of such mind were certain Goths, of whom it is written that, having in the spoil of a famous city taken a fair library, one hangman, belike fit to execute the fruits of their wits who had murdered a great number of bodies, would have set fire in it. "No," said another very gravely, "take heed what you do, for while they are busy about those toys, we shall with more leisure conquer their countries."[114] This indeed is the ordinary doctrine of ignorance and many words sometimes I have heard spent in it. But because this reason is generally against all learning as well as poetry (or rather all learning but poetry), because it were too large a digression to handle it, or at least too superfluous (since it is manifest that all government of action is to be gotten by knowledge, and knowledge best by gathering many knowledges, which is reading), I only, with Horace, to him that is of that opinion, "cheerfully bid him to remain foolish,"[115] for as for poetry itself, it is the freest from this objection, for poetry is the companion of camps. I dare undertake Orlando Furioso or honest King Arthur will never displease a soldier, but the "whatness" of "being" and "first matter"[116] will hardly agree with a corselet. And therefore, as I said in the beginning, even Turks and Tartars are delighted with poets.

Homer, a Greek, flourished before Greece flourished and, if to a slight conjecture a conjecture may be apposed, truly it may seem that as by him their learned men took almost their first light of knowledge, so their active men received their first motions of courage. Only Alexander's example may serve (who by Plutarch is

113. No . . . poetry: i.e., no memory is so ancient that poetry does not precede it.

114. Montaigne tells this story (*Essays*, I, 24).

115. *Jubeo stultum esse libenter* (Horace, *Satires*, I, i, 63, adapted).

116. Quiddity; *ens*; *prima materia*; all are scholastic philosophic terms.

accounted of such virtue that fortune was not his guide but his footstool), whose acts speak for him, though Plutarch did not (indeed the phoenix of war-like princes). This Alexander left his schoolmaster, living Aristotle, behind him but took dead Homer with him. He put the philosopher Callisthenes to death for his seeming philosophical—indeed mutinous—stubbornness, but the chief thing he was ever heard to wish for was that Homer had been alive. He well found he received more bravery of mind by the pattern of Achilles than by hearing the definition of fortitude. And therefore if Cato misliked Fulvius[117] for carrying Ennius with him to the field, it may be answered that, if Cato misliked it, the noble Fulvius liked it, or else he had not done it. For it was not the excellent Cato Uticensis (whose authority I would much more have reverenced) but it was the former, in truth a bitter punisher of faults, but else a man that had never sacrificed to the Graces. He misliked and cried out against all Greek learning and yet, being fourscore years old, began to learn it, belike fearing that Pluto understood not Latin. Indeed the Roman laws allowed no person to be carried to the wars but he that was in the soldiers' roll. And therefore, though Cato misliked his unmustered person, he misliked not his work, and if he had, Scipio Nasica (judged by common consent the best Roman) loved him. Both the other Scipio brothers, who had by their virtues no less surnames than of Asia and Africa, so loved him that they caused his body to be buried in their sepulcher.[118] So as Cato's authority, being but against his person and that answered with so far greater than himself, is herein of no validity.

But now indeed my burden is great, that Plato's name is laid upon me, whom, I must confess, of all philosophers I have ever esteemed most worthy of reverence, and with good reason, since of all

117. M. Fulvius Nobilior, conqueror of the Aetolians and consul (189 B.C.), took Ennius with him to Greece on his campaign.

118. Scipio Nasica was publicly acknowledged to be "best of the Romans" (Livy, *Histories*, XXIX, 8). His brothers, Scipio Africanus and Scipio Asiaticus, earned their titles by beating Hannibal at Zama (202 B.C.) and Antiochus III at Sipylus (190 B.C.). Cicero (*Pro Archia Poèta*, IX, 22) says only that Ennius's figure was carved on the family tomb of the Scipios; Boccaccio (*The Geneology of the Pagan Gods*, XIV, 4, 19) buries him there.

philosophers he is the most poetical. Yet if he will defile the fountain out of which his flowing streams have proceeded, let us boldly examine with what reasons he did it.

First, truly, a man might maliciously object that Plato, being a philosopher, was a natural enemy of poets, for indeed, after the philosophers had picked out of the sweet mysteries of poetry the right discerning true points of knowledge, they, forthwith putting it in method and making a school art of that which the poets did only teach by a divine delightfulness (beginning to spurn at their guides), like ungrateful prentices were not content to set up shop for themselves but sought all means to discredit their masters, which, by the force of delight being barred them, the less they could overthrow them, the more they hated them. For indeed they found for Homer, seven cities strove who should have him for their citizen, where many cities banished philosophers as not fit members to live among them. For only repeating certain of Euripides' verses,[119] many Athenians had their lives saved of the Syracusans, where the Athenians themselves thought many philosophers unworthy to live. Certain poets, as Simonides and Pindar,[120] had so prevailed with Hiero the First that of a tyrant they made him a just king, where Plato could do so little with Dionysius[121] that he himself, of a philosopher, was made a slave. But who should do thus, I confess, should requite the objections made against poets with like cavillations against philosophers, as likewise one should do that should bid one read *Phaedrus* or *Symposium*[122] in Plato or the discourse of love in Plutarch and see whether any poet do authorize abominable filthiness as they do.

Again, a man might ask out of what commonwealth Plato does banish them? In sooth, thence where he himself allows community of women, so as belike this banishment grew not for effeminate

119. This story about Euripides' verses comes from Plutarch, *Life of Nicias*, 29.

120. Simonides of Ceos (555–468 B.C.) reconciled Hiero, tyrant of Syracuse, and his brother, Theron.

121. Dionysius the Elder of Syracuse (430–367 B.C.) according to tradition gave Plato to a Spartan ambassador, who sold him as a slave.

122. Some sections of Plato's *Phaedrus* and *Symposium* can be read as encouraging homosexuality; Scaliger (*Poetices libri septem*, I, ii) so understands them, and objects to Plato.

wantonness, since little should poetical sonnets be hurtful when a man might have what woman he listed. But I honor philosophical instructions and bless the wits which bred them, so as they be not abused, which is likewise stretched to poetry. Saint Paul himself, who yet for the credit of poets alleges twice, two poets, and one of them by the name of a prophet,[123] sets a watchword upon philosophy—indeed, upon the abuse. So does Plato upon the abuse, not upon poetry. Plato found fault that the poets of his time filled the world with wrong opinions of the gods, making light tales of that unspotted essence, and therefore would not have the youth depraved with such opinions. Herein may much be said; let this suffice: the poets did not induce such opinions but did imitate those opinions already induced. For all the Greek stories can well testify that the very religion of that time stood upon many, and many-fashioned, gods, not taught so by poets but followed according to their nature of imitation. Who list may read in Plutarch the discourses of Isis and Osiris, of the cause why Oracles ceased, of the divine providence, and see whether the theology of that nation stood not upon such dreams, which the poets indeed superstitiously observed, and truly (since they had not the light of Christ) did much better in it than the philosophers who, shaking off superstition, brought in atheism.

Plato therefore (whose authority I had much rather justly construe than unjustly resist) meant not in general of poets in those words of which Julius Scaliger says, "by abuse of whose authority, barbarous and crude men wish to expel poets from the republic,"[124] but only meant to drive out those wrong opinions of the deity (whereof now, without further law, Christianity has taken away all

123. Who . . . prophet] *O;* omit *P.* St. Paul quotes Aratus and Cleanthes in Acts 17:28; "In him we live and move and have our being." Early commentators attribute Titus 1:12, "one of themselves, a prophet of their own said, Cretans are always liars, evil beasts, idle gluttons," to Epimenides (6th century B.C.). Paul may have had in mind the paradox "Epimenides the Cretan said that all Cretans are liars." 1 Corinthians 15:33, "Evil communications corrupt good manners," comes from Menander, *Thais.* St. Jerome in his commentary on the New Testament, Erasmus in his commentary, and Boccaccio (*Geneology,* XIV, 18) notice these poets. Paul warns against philosophy in Colossians 2:8.

124. *Qua authoritate barbari quidam atque hispidi abuti velint ad poetas ex republica exigendos* (Scaliger, *Poetices,* I, ii).

the hurtful belief) perchance, as he thought, nourished by then
esteemed poets. And a man need go no further than to Plato himself to know his meaning, who, in his dialogue called *Ion*, gives high
(and rightly) divine commendation unto poetry. So as Plato,
banishing the abuse, not the thing, not banishing it but giving due
honor to it, shall be our patron and not our adversary. For indeed I
had much rather (since truly I may do it) show their mistaking of
Plato, under whose lion's skin they would make an ass-like braying
against poesy, than go about to overthrow his authority (whom, the
wiser a man is, the more just cause he shall find to have in admiration), especially since he attributes unto poesy more than myself do,
namely, to be a very inspiring of a divine force, far above man's wit,
as in the forenamed dialogue is apparent.

Of the other side, who would show the honors have been by the
best sort of judgments granted them, a whole sea of examples would
present themselves: Alexanders, Caesars, Scipios, all favorers of
poets; Laelius (called the Roman Socrates) himself a poet (so as
part of *Heautontimoroumenon* in Terence was supposed to be made by
him);[125] and even the Greek Socrates (whom Apollo confirmed
to be the only wise man) is said to have spent part of his old time in
putting Aesop's fables into verses (and therefore full evil should
it become his scholar Plato to put such words in his master's mouth
against poets).[126] But what needs more? Aristotle writes the art of
poesy, and why, if it should not be written? Plutarch teaches the use
to be gathered of them, and how, if they should not be read? And
who reads Plutarch's either history or philosophy shall find he trims
both their garments with guards[127] of poesy. But I list not to
defend poesy with the help of his underling, historiography. Let it
suffice to have showed it is a fit soil for praise to dwell upon, and
what dispraise may set upon it is either easily overcome or transformed into just commendation.

125. Gaius Laelius (2nd century B.C.) was a friend of the Scipios. Cicero (*Offices*,
I, xxvi, 90) compared his philosophic equanimity to Socrates' and said that some
people attributed Terence's comedies to Laelius (*Epistles to Atticus*, VII, iii).

126. Plato (*Apology*, 21A) says that the Delphic Oracle replied "no" when
asked if any man were wiser than Socrates. He also says (*Phaedo*, 60D) that
Socrates versified Aesop.

127. Guards: decorations, gauds.

So that since the excellencies of it may be so easily and so justly confirmed and the low-creeping objections so soon trodden down, it not being an art of lies, but of true doctrine; not of effeminateness, but of notable stirring of courage; not of abusing man's wit, but of strengthening man's wit; not banished but honored by Plato, let us rather plant more laurels for to engarland the poets' heads (which honor of being laureate, as besides them only triumphant captains were, is a sufficient authority to show the price they ought to be held in) than suffer the ill-savored breath of such wrong speakers once to blow upon the clear springs of poesy.

[*Digressio*]

But since I have run so long a career in this matter, methinks before I give my pen a full stop it shall be but a little more lost time to enquire why England, the mother of excellent minds, should be grown so hard a stepmother to poets (who certainly in wit ought to pass all others since all only proceeds from their wit, being indeed makers of themselves, not takers of others). How can I but exclaim, "Muse, help me remember the reasons, and what heavenly power was enraged?"[128] Sweet poesy, that has anciently had kings, emperors, senators, great captains, such as (besides a thousand others) David, Hadrian, Sophocles, Germanicus, not only to favor poets but to be poets, and of our nearer times can present for her patrons a Robert, King of Sicily, the great King Francis of France, King James of Scotland; such cardinals as Bembus and Bibbiena; such famous preachers and teachers as Bèza and Melanchthon; so learned philosophers as Fracastorius and Scaliger; so great orators as Pontanus and Muretus; so piercing wits as George Buchanan; so grave counselors as (besides many but before all) that Hospital of France[129] (than whom, I think, that realm never brought forth a

---

128. *Musa mihi causas memoria quo numine laeso* (Virgil, *Aeneid*, I, 12).

129. Hadrian (Emperor, A.D. 117–138) was author of a poem to his soul beginning, "*animula, vagula, blandula.*" The playwright Sophocles was one of the ten generals appointed against Samos (440 B.C.). Germanicus Caesar (15 B.C.–A.D. 19) conquered the Germans and reputedly translated the *Phaenomena* of Aratus. Robert of Anjou (1275–1343) was Petrarch's patron. Francis I of France (1494–1547) was a patron of Erasmus, Estienne, and Marot. James VI of Scotland

more accomplished judgment more firmly builded upon virtue),
I say these, with numbers of others, not only to read others' poesies
but to poetize for others' readings—that poesy, thus embraced in all
other places, should only find in our time a hard welcome in
England, I think the very earth laments it and therefore decks our
soil with fewer laurels than it was accustomed.

For heretofore, poets have in England also flourished and (which
is to be noted) even in those times when the trumpet of Mars did
sound loudest. And now that an over-faint quietness should seem to
strew the house for poets, they are almost in as good reputation as
the mountebanks at Venice. Truly even that, as of the one side it
gives great praise to poesy which, like Venus but to better purpose,
had rather be troubled in the net with Mars than enjoy the homely
quiet of Vulcan, so serves it for a piece of a reason why they are less
grateful to idle England, which now can scarce endure the pain of a
pen. Upon this necessarily follows that base men with servile wits
undertake it, who think it enough if they can be rewarded of the
printer. And so, as Epaminondas is said with the honor of his virtue
to have made an office, by his exercising it, which before was

---

(James I of England) translated Du Bartas's *Urania*. Sidney could have read in
Buchanan's *Rerum scoticorum historia* that James I of Scotland (1394–1437) wrote
poetry. Pietro Bembo (1470–1547), a cardinal and humanist at the Medici court,
was a famous Ciceronian. Bernardo Dovizio, Cardinal Bibbiena (1470–1520), was
Lorenzo Medici's secretary and author of the Plautine comedy, *La Calandria*.
Théodore de Bèze (1519–1605) was a Calvinist scholar, preacher, and leader; he
wrote Biblical poetry and translated the New Testament. Philipp Melanchthon
(1497–1560) was an associate of Luther's, a professor of Greek at Wittenberg, and a
friend of Sidney's friend, Languet. Girolamo Fracastoro (1483–1553) was a
humanist, naturalist, and philosopher; he wrote *Syphilis*, *Naugerius*, and *Turrius*.
His *Naugerius* is, like Sidney's *Defense*, a mixture of Neo-Platonist and Aristotelian
literary theory. Julius Caesar Scaliger (1484–1558) wrote *Poetices libri septem* and
Latin poetry. Giovanni Pontano (1426–1503) was a diplomat, scholar, soldier,
President of the Academy of Naples, and author of the astronomical poem *Urania*.
Marc Antoine Muret (1526–1585) was a humanist and colleague of Buchanan in
Paris; he wrote hymns and other poetry. George Buchanan (1506–1582) was
a Scottish poet and scholar; he tutored James I of England and was a friend of
many of Sidney's Protestant humanist friends. Michel de L'Hôpital (1507–1573)
was Chancellor of France and wrote poetry.

contemptible to become highly respected,[130] so these men, no more but setting their names to it, by their own disgracefulness disgrace the most graceful poesy. For now, as if all the Muses were got with child to bring forth bastard poets, without any commission they do post[131] over the banks of Helicon till they make the readers more weary than post-horses, while in the meantime they "whose hearts the Titan moulded out of better clay"[132] are better content to suppress the out-flowings of their wit than, by publishing them, to be accounted knights of the same order.

But I, that before ever I durst aspire unto the dignity, am admitted into the company of the paper-blurrers, do find the very true cause of our wanting estimation is want of desert, taking upon us to be poets in despite of Pallas. Now wherein we want desert were a thankworthy labor to express. But if I knew, I should have mended myself. But as I never desired the title, so have I neglected the means to come by it, only, overmastered by some thoughts, I yielded an inky tribute unto them.

Marry, they that delight in poesy itself should seek to know what they do and how they do, and especially look themselves in an unflattering glass of reason if they be inclinable unto it, for poesy must not be drawn by the ears. It must be gently led, or rather it must lead, which was partly the cause that made the ancient learned affirm it was a divine gift and no human skill, since all other knowledges lie ready for any that have strength of wit. A poet, no industry can make, if his own genius be not carried into it, and therefore is it[133] an old proverb, "Orators are made, poets are born."[134]

Yet confess I always that, as the fertilest ground must be manured, so must the highest flying wit have a Daedalus to guide him. That

130. Epaminondas (4th century B.C.) was a Theban statesman and general. Plutarch (*Moralia*, X, v, 811B–D) relates that he dignified the office of telmarch, which, before he held it, was despised, since it was the office of street commissioner and refuse collector.

131. post] *O;* pass *P.*

132. *Queis meliore luto finxit praecordia Titan* (Juvenal, *Satires,* XIV, 34–35, adapted).

133. it] *O; omit P.*

134. *Orator fit, poeta nascitur.*

Daedalus they say (both in this and in other) has three wings to bear itself up into the air of due commendation: that is, art, imitation, and exercise. But these neither artificial rules nor imitative patterns we much cumber ourselves withal. Exercise indeed we do, but that very fore-backwardly, for where we should exercise to know, we exercise as having known, and so is our brain delivered of much matter which never was begotten by knowledge. For there being two principal parts, matter to be expressed by words and words to express the matter, in neither we use art or imitation rightly. Our matter is "what you will,"[135] indeed (though wrongly) performing Ovid's verse, "whatever I tryd to say will come out verse,"[136] never marshaling it into any assured rank, that (almost) the readers cannot tell where to find themselves.

Chaucer undoubtedly did excellently in his *Troilus and Criseyde*, of whom truly I know not whether to marvel more either that he in that misty time could see so clearly or that we in this clear age walk[137] so stumblingly after him. Yet had he great wants, fit to be forgiven in so reverend an antiquity. I account the *Mirror of Magistrates* meetly furnished of beautiful parts, and in the Earl of Surrey's lyrics,[138] many things tasting of a noble birth and worthy of a noble mind. *The Shepherd's Calendar* has much poetry in his eclogues, indeed worthy the reading if I be not deceived. That same framing of his style to an old rustic language I dare not allow since neither Theocritus[139] in Greek, Virgil in Latin, nor Sannazaro in Italian did affect it. Besides these, I do not remember to have seen but few (to speak boldly) printed that have poetical sinews in them. For proof whereof, let but most of the verses be put in prose and then ask the meaning, and it will be found that one verse did but beget another, without ordering at the first what should be at the last, which becomes a confused mass of words with a ting-ling sound of rhyme barely accompanied with reasons.

135. *Quodlibet.*

136. *Quicquid conabor dicere, versus erat* (Ovid, *Tristia*, IV, x, 26, adapted).

137. walk] *O;* go *P.*

138. *The Mirror for Magistrates* contained a series of exemplary tragedies in which Princes could theoretically recognize their vices and correct them; it was often reprinted. Henry Howard, Earl of Surrey (1517?–1547): his poems appeared in *Tottel's Miscellany* (1557).

139. Theocritus (3rd century B.C.) wrote eclogues.

Our tragedies and comedies (not without cause cried out against) observing rules neither of honest civility nor skilful poetry, excepting *Gorboduc* (again I say of those that I have seen) which, notwithstanding as it is full of stately speeches and well-sounding phrases, climbing to the height of Seneca's style,[140] and as full of notable morality which it does most delightfully teach and so obtain the very end of poesy, yet in truth it is very defectious in the circumstances (which grieves me because it might not remain as an exact model of all tragedies). For it is faulty both in place and time, the two necessary companions of all corporal actions. For where the stage should always represent but one place and the uttermost time presupposed in it should be (both by Aristotle's precept[141] and common reason) but one day, there is both many days and places inartificially[142] imagined.

But if it be so in *Gorboduc*, how much more in all the rest where you shall have Asia of the one side and Africa of the other, and so many other under-kingdoms that the player when he comes in must ever begin with telling where he is, or else the tale will not be conceived. Now you shall have three ladies walk to gather flowers and then we must believe the stage to be a garden. By and by we hear news of shipwreck in the same place. Then we are to blame if we accept it not for a rock. Upon the back of that comes out a hideous monster with fire and smoke, and then the miserable beholders are bound to take it for a cave, while in the meantime two armies fly in, represented with four swords and bucklers, and then what hard heart will not receive it for a pitched field?

Now of time they are much more liberal. For ordinary it is that two young princes fall in love, after many traverses she is got with child, delivered of a fair boy, he is lost, grows a man, falls in love and is ready to get another child, and all this in two hours' space (which, how absurd it is in sense, even sense may imagine and art has taught

140. *Gorboduc*, by Thomas Sackville and Thomas Norton (who translated Calvin's *Institutes*), was presented before Elizabeth in 1561; it is modeled on the tragedies of Seneca. L. Annaeus Seneca (5 B.C.?–A.D. 65) was a stoic philosopher, tutor to Nero, who wrote moralized rhetorical tragedies much admired during the Renaissance. Sidney praises him in standard terms, which he might have found in Scaliger, *Poetices*, VI, vi.

141. *Poetics*, V, 1449b.

142. Inartificially: unartfully.

and all ancient examples justified, and at this day the ordinary players in Italy will not err in).[143] Yet will some bring in an example of *Eunuch* in Terence that contains matter of two days (yet far short of twenty years). True it is, and so was it to be played in two days, and so fitted to the time it set forth. And though Plautus have in one place done amiss, let us hit it with him, and not miss with him. But they will say, "How then shall we set forth a story which contains both many places and many times?" And do they not know that a tragedy is tied to the laws of poesy and not of history; not bound to follow the story but having liberty either to feign a quite new matter or to frame the history to the most tragical convenience? Again, many things may be told which cannot be showed, if they know the difference between reporting and representing. As for example, I may speak (though I am here) of Peru and in speech digress from that to the description of Calcutta,[144] but in action I cannot represent it without Pacolet's horse. And so was the manner the ancients took, by some *nuntius*[145] to recount things done in former time or other place.

Lastly, if they will represent a history, they must not (as Horace says) begin "with the egg,"[146] but they must come to the principal point of that one action which they will represent. By example this will be best expressed. I have a story of young Polydorus, delivered for safety's sake with great riches by his father Priam to Polymnestor, King of Thrace, in the Trojan war time. He, after some years, hearing the overthrow of Priam, for to make the treasure his own, murders the child. The body of the child is taken up by Hecuba. She[147] the same day finds a sleight to be revenged most cruelly of the tyrant. Where now would one of our tragedy writers begin but with the delivery of the child? Then should he sail over into Thrace and so spend I know not how many years, and travel numbers of places.

143. How absurd . . . err in: i.e., all ancient examples . . . have proved how absurd it is, and even the Italian actors don't violate the rule.

144. Calcutta] Calicut *P, O.*

145. Pacolet was a magician in the romance *Valentine and Orson.* A *nuntius* is a messenger.

146. *Ab ovo* (Horace, *Art of Poetry*, l. 147).

147. up by Hecuba, she] *O;* up. Hecuba, she *P.*

But where does Euripides? Even with the finding of the body, the rest leaving to be told by the spirit of Polydorus. This needs no further to be enlarged. The dullest wit may conceive it.

But besides these gross absurdities, how all their plays be neither right tragedies nor right comedies, mingling kings and clowns, not because the matter so carries it but thrust in the clown by head and shoulders to play a part in majestical matters with neither decency nor discretion, so as neither the admiration and commiseration nor the right sportfulness is by their mongrel tragicomedy obtained. I know Apuleius did somewhat so, but that is a thing recounted with space of time, not represented in one moment, and I know the ancients have one or two examples of tragicomedies, as Plautus has *Amphytrio*. But if we mark them well, we shall find that they never (or very daintily) match hornpipes and funerals.

So falls it out that, having indeed no right comedy in that comical part of our tragedy, we have nothing but scurrility unworthy of any chaste ears or some extreme show of doltishness, indeed fit to lift up a loud laughter and nothing else, where the whole tract of a comedy should be full of delight, as the tragedy should be still maintained in a well-raised admiration. But our comedians think there is no delight without laughter, which is very wrong, for though laughter may come with delight, yet comes it not of delight, as though delight should be the cause of laughter (but well may one thing breed both together). Nay, rather in themselves they have, as it were, a kind of contrariety, for delight we scarcely do but in things that have a conveniency to ourselves or to the general nature; laughter almost ever comes of things most disproportioned to ourselves and nature. Delight has a joy in it either permanent or present; laughter has only a scornful tickling. For example, we are ravished with delight to see a fair woman, and yet are far from being moved to laughter. We laugh at deformed creatures wherein certainly we cannot delight. We delight in good chances, we laugh at mischances. We delight to hear the happiness of our friends and country at which he were worthy to be laughed at that would laugh. We shall, contrarily, laugh sometimes to find a matter quite mistaken and go down the hill against the bias; in the mouth of some such men as for the respect of them one shall be heartily sorry yet[148] he cannot choose but laugh and so is rather pained than delighted with laughter.[149] Yet deny I not but that they may go well together, for as in Alexander's picture well set out we delight without laughter, and in twenty mad antics we laugh without delight, so in Hercules, painted with his great beard and furious countenance in a woman's attire spinning at Omphale's commandment, it breeds both delight and laughter, for the representing of so strange a power in love procures delight, and the scornfulness of the action stirs laughter.

But I speak to this purpose, that all the end of the comical part be not upon such scornful matters as stir laughter only but mix with it that delightful teaching which is the end of poesy. And the great fault even in that point of laughter (and forbidden plainly by Aristotle)[150] is that they stir laughter in sinful things (which are rather execrable than ridiculous) or in miserable (which are rather to be pitied than scorned). For what is it to make folks gape at a wretched beggar and a beggarly clown or, against law of hospitality, to jest at strangers because they speak not English so well as we do (what do we learn, since it is certain "poverty has nothing in itself harder to bear than that it makes men ridiculous")?[151] But rather a busy loving courtier and a heartless threatening Thraso, a self-wise-seeming schoolmaster, a wry transformed traveler—these (if we saw walk in stage-names) which we play naturally—therein were delightful laughter and teaching delightfulness: as in the other, the tragedies of Buchanan do justly bring forth a divine admiration.[152]

148. yet] *O; omit P.*
149. We shall . . . bias . . . laughter: In the game of bowls, the ball moves in a predictable curving path towards its target because of a bias or irregularity in the shape of the ball. If the ball were to move in the direction opposite to that imparted by the bias, as it would when the ground sloped in the wrong direction, comedy might result. Sidney means here that a dignified man, deserving respect, might misspeak so ridiculously as to force us to laugh, although the laughter would pain us, since we respect the speaker.
150. *Ethics,* IV, 8, 1128a; see also *Poetics,* V, 1449a.
151. *Nil habet infelix paupertas durius in se/ Quam quod ridiculos homines facit* (Juvenal, *Satires,* III, 152–153).
152. Sidney previously paired admiration, appropriate to tragedy, and delight,

But I have lavished out too many words of this play-matter. I do it because, as they are excelling parts of poesy, so is there none so much used in England and none can be more pitifully abused, which, like an unmannerly daughter showing a bad education, causes her mother Poesy's honesty to be called in question.

Other sorts of poetry almost have we none but that lyrical kind of songs and sonnets which, Lord, if he gave us so good minds, how well it might be employed (and with how heavenly fruits both private and public) in singing the praises of the immortal beauty, the immortal goodness of that God who gives us hands to write and wits to conceive, of which we might well want words but never matter, of which we could turn our eyes to nothing but we should ever have new-budding occasions. But truly many of such writings as come under the banner of unresistable love, if I were a mistress, would never persuade me they were in love, so coldly they apply fiery speeches, as men that had rather read lovers' writings (and so caught up certain swelling phrases which hang together, like a man that once told me the wind was at Northwest and by South because he would be sure to name winds enough) than that in truth they feel those passions (which easily, as I think, may be bewrayed by that same forcibleness or *Energia*, as the Greeks call it, of the writer). But let this be a sufficient though short note that we miss the right use of the material point of poesy.

Now, for the outside of it which is words or (as I may term it) diction, it is even well worse, so is that[153] honey-flowing matron Eloquence appareled, or rather disguised, in a courtesan-like painted affectation: one time with so far-fetched words that many seem monsters but must seem strangers to any poor Englishman; another time with coursing of a letter, as if they were bound to follow the method of a dictionary; another time with figures and flowers extremely winter-starved.

---

appropriate to comedy. He here mentions an existing example of well-raised admiration to balance his hypothetical comic example of natural comic parts which men act out in life and would delight to see on the stage, since the parts are convenient to the general nature. Buchanan wrote four tragedies, two on classical themes, *Medea* and *Alcestis*, and two on Biblical themes, *Jepthes* and *Baptistes*.

153. So is that] *O;* so is it that *P*.

But I would this fault were only peculiar to versifiers and had not as large possession among prose printers and (which is to be marveled) among many scholars and (which is to be pitied) among some preachers. Truly I could wish (if at least I might be so bold to wish in a thing beyond the reach of my capacity) the diligent imitators of Tully and Demosthenes (most worthy to be imitated) did not so much keep Nizolian paper-books of their figures and phrases as by attentive translation, as it were, devour them whole and make them wholly theirs. For now they cast sugar and spice upon every dish that is served to the table (like those Indians, not content to wear earrings at the fit and natural place of the ears, but they will thrust jewels through their nose and lips because they will be sure to be fine). Tully, when he was to drive out Catiline, as it were, with a thunderbolt of eloquence, often uses the figure of repetition, as "He lives? He lives! Still to the Senate! He still comes! He comes to the Senate!"[154] and so forth. Indeed, inflamed with a well-grounded rage, he would have his words, as it were, double out of his mouth and so do that artificially which we see men in choler do naturally. And we, having noted the grace of those words, hale them in sometimes to a familiar epistle, when it were too much choler to be choleric.[155] How well store of similar cadences[156] does sound with the gravity of the pulpit I would but invoke Demosthenes' soul to tell, who with a rare daintiness uses them. Truly, they have made me think of the sophister that with too much subtlety would prove two eggs three and, though he might be counted a sophister, had none for his labor.[157] So these men, bringing in such a kind of eloquence, well may they obtain an opinion of a seeming fineness but persuade few, which should be the end of their fineness.

154. *Vivit! vivit? immo in senatum? venit immo? in senatum venit!* from *hic tamen vivit, Vivit? Immo vero etiam in senatum venit* (Cicero, *Against Catiline*, I, i, 2).

155. Sidney puns on "choler," rage, and "color," rhetorical device.

156. Similar cadences: *similiter cadentia*, a Latin rhetorical term for members in which words end similarly, a sort of internal rhyme.

157. Sidney refers to a joke used in medieval logic courses to illustrate distinctions between name and thing. A logic student made two eggs into three by naming the first "one" and the second "two" and adding to get three. His peasant interlocutor ate "one" and "two" and told him he might eat "three" himself for his lunch.

Now, for similitudes in certain printed discourses, I think all herbarists, all stories of beasts, fowls, and fishes are rifled up that they may come in multitudes to wait upon any of our conceits, which certainly is as absurd a surfeit to the ears as is possible. For the force of a similitude not being to prove anything to a contrary disputer but only to explain to a willing hearer, when that is done the rest is a most tedious prattling, rather overswaying the memory from the purpose whereto they were applied than any whit informing the judgment already either satisfied, or by similitudes not to be satisfied.

For my part, I do not doubt when Antonius and Crassus (the great forefathers of Cicero in eloquence), the one (as Cicero testifies of them) pretended not to know art, the other not to set by it, because with a plain sensibleness they might win credit of popular ears (which credit is the nearest step to persuasion, which persuasion is the chief mark of oratory)—I do not doubt, I say, but that they used these knacks very sparingly (which who does generally use, any man may see does dance to his own music and so [158] be noted by the audience more careful to speak curiously than truly). Undoubtedly (at least to my opinion undoubtedly) I have found in diverse small-learned courtiers a more sound style than in some professors of learning, of which I can guess no other cause but that the courtier, following that which by practice he finds fittest to nature, therein (though he know it not) does according to art though not by art, where the other, using art to show art and not hide art (as in these cases he should do), flies from nature and indeed abuses art.

But what? Methinks I deserve to be pounded for straying from poetry to oratory. But both have such an affinity in the wordish consideration that I think this digression will make my meaning receive the fuller understanding, which is not to take upon me to teach poets how they should do but only, finding myself sick among the rest, to show some one or two spots of the common infection grown among the most part of writers, that, acknowledging ourselves somewhat awry, we may bend to the right use both of matter and manner.

158. so] to *P; omit O.*

Whereto our language gives us great occasion, being indeed capable of any excellent exercising of it. I know some will say it is a mingled language. And why not? So much the better, taking the best of both the other. Another will say it wants grammar. Nay, truly, it has that praise that it wants not grammar, for grammar it might have but it needs it not, being so easy in itself and so void of those cumbersome differences of cases, genders, moods, and tenses (which I think was a piece of the Tower of Babylon's curse, that a man should be put to school to learn his mother-tongue). But for the uttering sweetly and properly the conceit of the mind (which is the end of speech), that has it equally with any other tongue in the world, and is particularly happy in compositions of two or three words together, near the Greek, far beyond the Latin, which is one of the greatest beauties can be in a language.

Now of versifying there are two sorts, the one ancient, the other modern. The ancient marked the quantity of each syllable and according to that framed his verse. The modern, observing only number (with some regard of the accent), the chief life of it stands in that like sounding of the words which we call rhyme. Whether of these be the more excellent would bear many speeches, the ancient no doubt more fit for music (both words and time observing quantity) and more fit lively to express diverse passions by the low or lofty sound of the well-weighed syllable. The latter likewise with his rhyme strikes a certain music to the ear, and, in fine, since it does delight (though by another way) it obtains the same purpose, there being in either sweetness and wanting in neither majesty.

Truly, the English, before any vulgar language I know, is fit for both sorts. For, for the ancient, the Italian is so full of vowels that it must ever be cumbered with elisions, the Dutch so of the other side with consonants that they cannot yield the sweet sliding fit for a verse. The French, in his whole language, has not one word that has his accent in the last syllable saving two, called *antepenultima*, and little more has the Spanish, and therefore very gracelessly may they use dactyls. The English is subject to none of these defects.

Now for rhyme, though we do not observe quantity, yet we observe the accent very precisely, which other languages either cannot do or will not do so absolutely. That *caesura*, or breathing place in the midst of the verse, neither Italian nor Spanish have; the French and we never almost fail of. Lastly, even the very rhyme itself, the Italian cannot put it in the last syllable (by the French named the masculine rhyme) but still in the next to the last (which the French call the female) or the next before that (which the Italians term[159] *sdrucciola*). The example of the former is *buono*, *suono*, of the *sdrucciola* is *femina*, *semina*. The French, of the other side, has both the male (as *bon*, *son*) and the female (as *plaise*, *taise*), but the *sdrucciola* he has not, where the English has all three (as *due-true*, *father-rather*, *motion-potion*) with much more which might be said but that already I find the trifling of this discourse is much too much enlarged.

[*Peroratio*]

So that since the ever praiseworthy poesy is full of virtue-breeding delightfulness and void of no gift that ought to be in the noble name of learning; since the blames laid against it are either false or feeble; since the cause why it is not esteemed in England is the fault of poet-apes, not poets; since, lastly, our tongue is most fit to honor poesy and to be honored by poesy, I conjure you all that have had the evil luck to read this ink-wasting toy of mine, even in the name of the nine Muses, no more to scorn the sacred mysteries of poesy; no more to laugh at the name of poets as though they were next inheritors to fools; no more to jest at the reverend title of a rhymer, but to believe with Aristotle that they were the ancient treasurers of the Grecians' divinity; to believe with Bembus that they were first bringers-in of all civility; to believe with Scaliger that no philosopher's precepts can sooner make you an honest man than the reading of Virgil;[160] to believe with Clauserus, the translator of Cornutus, that it pleased the heavenly deity by Hesiod and Homer, under the veil of fables to give us all knowledge, logic, rhetoric, philosophy natural and moral (and what not?);[161] to believe with me that there are many mysteries contained in poetry

159. term] *O; omit P.*
160. Scaliger, *Poetices*, III, xix.
161. Cornutus (1st century A.D.) was a stoic philosopher, and the teacher of Persius. What not: *Quid non.*

which of purpose were written darkly lest by profane wits it should be abused; to believe with Landino that they are so beloved of the gods that whatsover they write proceeds of a divine fury; lastly, to believe themselves when they tell you they will make you immortal by their verses.

Thus doing, your name shall flourish in the printers' shops. Thus doing, you shall be of kin to many a poetical preface. Thus doing, you shall be most fair, most rich, most wise, most all. You shall dwell upon superlatives. Thus doing, though you be "born of a slave-born father" you shall suddenly grow "kin with Hercules," "if my verses can do it." [162] Thus doing, your soul shall be placed with Dante's Beatrice or Virgil's Anchises.

But if (fie of such a but) you be born so near the dull-making cataract of Nilus that you cannot hear the planet-like music of poetry; [163] if you have so earth-creeping a mind that it cannot lift itself up to look to the sky of poetry, or rather by a certain rustical disdain will become such a mome as to be a Momus of poetry, then, though I will not wish unto you the ass's ears of Midas, nor to be driven by a poet's verses, as Bubonax was, to hang himself, [164] nor to be rhymed to death as is said to be done in Ireland, yet thus much curse I must send you in the behalf of all poets, that while you live, you live in love and never get favor for lacking skill of a sonnet, and when you die, your memory die from the earth for want of an epitaph.

162. *Libertine patre natus* (Horace, *Satires*, I, vi, 6). *Herculea proles* has no particular source. *Si quid mea carmina possunt* (Virgil, *Aeneid*, IX, 446).

163. The cataract of the Nile is deafening in *Scipio's Dream*, part of Cicero's *De Re Publica*, VI, xviii, 18–19. Macrobius's commentary allegorizes this deafness as the worldly man's inability to hear the heavenly music of the Neo-Platonist spheres.

164. Momus, the type of the satirist and carping critic, was the mythical son of Night and Obscurity; Jupiter threw him out of Olympus for his misguided and malicious mockery. Midas, legendary king of Phrygia, judged Pan's music better than Apollo's, and was punished with donkey's ears (Ovid, *Metamorphoses*, XI 146–180). Hipponax, an Iambic poet, was caricatured by Bupalus and Athenis, and wrote poems that so shamed them that they committed suicide; Archilocus wrote the same kind of poetry against Lycambes and his daughters. Sidney, working from memory, merged Hipponax and Bupalus into Bubonax, and has Archilocus in mind as well.

Supplementary Notes

In the parentheses preceding each note, the number preceding the colon refers to the page; that following the colon refers to the line or lines on the page. The bracketed indications of rhetorical divisions (*Exordium*, *Narratio*, etc.) in the text are not counted in the line numbering.

(4:9) The complaint that people undervalue poetry is a humanist commonplace. Spenser in his "October" Eclogue in the *Shepherd's Calendar*, Boccaccio in *The Geneology of the Pagan Gods* (XIV, 1–5), and George Puttenham in *The Art of English Poesy* (ed. G. D. Willcock and A. Walker [Cambridge: Cambridge University Press, 1936], pp. 16 ff.), make essentially the same complaint. For a fuller list see G. Shepherd, ed., *An Apology for Poetry*, by Sir Philip Sidney (London: Nelson, 1965), p. 145.

(4:12) Plato, *Republic*, X, banished the poets. He requested (*Rep.* X, 607 D) that someone defend them: "I propose then, that she be allowed to return from exile, but upon this condition only—that she make a defence of herself in lyrical or some other metre. . . . And we may further grant to those of her defenders who are lovers of poetry and yet not poets the permission to speak in prose on her behalf. . . . If her defence fails, then . . . must we . . . give her up, though not without a struggle" (Plato, *Dialogues*, ed. & tr. B. Jowett [London, 1892], III, 323). Sidney is careful to claim that he is not a poet, and thus his defense in prose acts as a response to Plato's request. Humanist defenders usually felt that they had to explain Plato's banishment of poets (Bernard Weinberg, *A History of Literary Criticism in the Italian Renaissance* [Chicago: University of Chicago Press, 1961], pp. 250 ff.).

(5:5) The arguments which Sidney advances here and in the preceding paragraph are humanist commonplaces (Weinberg,

Literary Criticism, pp. 254–257, 263–267, 642–643). They go back to commentators on Horace (*Art of Poetry*, ll. 391 ff.) on the one hand, and to Augustine (*City of God*, XVIII, 14) and Boccaccio (*Geneology*, XIV, 8) on the other. Sidney's list of philosophic poets seems to have come from Julius Caesar Scaliger (*Poetices libri septem*, I, ii), but he could also have derived such a list from Jean de Serre's (Serranus) commentary on Plato's *Ion* (J. Serranus, ed., *Platonis Opera* [1578], I, 529). The fullest account of these mythic poets as seen by the humanists is Juan Luis Vives' in his notes to Augustine, *City of God*, tr. J. H. (1610), pp. 687 ff.

(6:15) The opinion that Plato is an allegorist and poet goes back at least to Quintilian (*Institutes*, V, xi, 39). Humanist and Neo-Platonist critics echoed it continuously through the Renaissance. W. A. Ringler, Jr., outlines the history of the opinion (Ringler, ed., *Oratio in laudem artis poeticae*, by John Rainolds [Princeton: Princeton University Press, 1940], p. 74). Critics identified Plato's allegory as poetic (Serranus, *Platonis Opera*, I, **6^v; Scaliger, *Poetices*, III, lxxxiv) as well as his narrative framework. Plato sets the *Symposium* at a banquet and the *Phaedrus* in the country, and uses the story of Gyge's ring in the *Republic*, II, 359. Cicero repeats it in *Offices*, III, ix, 38–39.

(7:25) The prophetic powers attributed to Virgil during the Middle Ages and the Renaissance seem to derive from commentaries on Eclogue IV, which credit Virgil with having dimly prophesied the birth of Christ. Landino's commentary on Dante's *Divine Comedy* and his *Disputationes Camuldulenses*, III and IV, summarize such opinion. Hermetic speculation extended this prophetic power to Orpheus (Frances A. Yates, *Giordano Bruno and the Hermetic Tradition* [Chicago: University of Chicago Press, 1964], p. 78). Other human-ists extended such a prophetic power to Ennius (Aldo S. Bernardo, *Petrarch, Scipio and the "Africa"* [Baltimore: Johns Hopkins Press, 1962], pp. 43–46). Renaissance commentators usually attributed this prophetic power to the inspiration of the poet's frenzy (Baxter Hathaway, *The Age of Criticism* [Ithaca: Cornell University Press, 1962], pp. 431–436).

(8:2) Sidney, throughout the *Defense*, denies the theory of the poet's frenzy. He follows Boccaccio (*Geneology*, **XIV**, 8) and discriminates between the direct inspiration of God which moved David to sing, and the natural force of inbreathed reason which inspired the poet to a semi-prophetic perception of the golden world of prelapsarian virtue.

(8:5) The argument that the Psalms were poetry was commonplace. English critics used it often (I. Baroway, "The Bible as Poetry in the English Renaissance: an Introduction," *Journal of English and Germanic Philology*, **XXXII** [1933], pp. 447–480; I. Baroway, "The Hebrew Hexameter: a Study in Renaissance Sources and Interpretation," *E.L.H.*, II [1935], pp. 66–91; G. G. Smith, ed., *Elizabethan Critical Essays* [Oxford: Clarendon Press, 1904], I, 71; II, 10, 207). Ringler traces the argument through Boccaccio and Bede to Jerome (Ringler, *Oratio*, p. 74). Sidney could have found it in F. Junius and I. Tremellius, "Praefatio," *Bibliorum Pars Tertia* (1580), pp. 3–6. Junius and Tremellius classify Job, Psalms, Proverbs, Ecclesiastes, and the Song of Songs as the poetical books of the Bible. The Pléiade in France made translation of the Psalms part of its program of divine poetry. Frances A. Yates, *French Academies of the Sixteenth Century* (London: Warburg, 1947), pp. 199–217, argues that the Pléiade translators of Psalms and authors of divine poetry hoped to use the spiritual power they attributed to such poetry to effect a conciliation between the warring Protestants and Catholics.

(8:10) Sidney distinguishes here between verse and profitable fiction as the earmark of poetry. I. Baroway studies Sidney's distinction in "Tremellius, Sidney, and Biblical Verse," *MLN*, **XLIX** (1934), pp. 145–149. Jerome, Epistle LIII, and Josephus, *Antiquities of the Jews*, VII, xii, 3, 305, had discussed the meter of the Psalms, and Renaissance critics followed them. Sidney, emphasizing profitable fiction rather than meter, directs attention to the poet's perception rather than his form, and prepares for his distinction between David's direct inspiration and the inspiration of the "right" poet, which, in turn, makes a place for the "right" poet in the Church of God.

(8:24) Sidney could have found this argument, based on the

Greek name, in Scaliger, *Poetices*, I, i–ii. It is a commonplace argument, however. Renaissance scholarly commentators usually began their comments with a more or less fanciful investigation of the name of the topic or genre upon which they were commenting and tried to derive hints of the nature of the being from the etymology of the name. These commentaries were usually eclectic. For example de Serre, although a Ficinian commentator on Plato, refers his reader to the Aristotelian Scaliger (Serranus, *Platonis Opera*, I, 528–529).

(9:16) Sidney follows Scaliger's line of argument in *Poetices*, I, i. He uses the subordination of an art to the material which nature provides (Aristotle, *Physics*, II, 2, 194a) to contrast with the freedom of poetry from this subordination to a "second" or fallen nature. The Aristotelian distinction is common. Shepherd, ed., *Apology*, p. 153, lists other appearances of the argument.

(9:28) Here Sidney uses available critical theory in a novel combination. He draws his illustrations in this paragraph from Horace, *Art of Poetry*, ll. 1–13, but modifies the Horatian tradition of commentary. Commentators on Horace tended to derive such forms as centaurs from the operation of the fantasy. Sidney adapts these Horatian examples to the Aristotelian description of art as subordinate to nature. He uses this adaptation, as some other commentators used Aristotle's distinctions, to answer Plato's attack by using an argument drawn from Aristotle (Weinberg, *Literary Criticism*, p. 347). Sidney, for example, relates the image of the centaurs (which rhetorically inclined commentators identified as a form of phantasmata) to Aristotle's verisimilar and probable, and to Plato's Ideas. Other critics had combined the verisimilar and the Ideas. Hathaway, *Age of Criticism*, pp. 129–159, demonstrates the process which led to this assimilation. Sidney then subsumes the combination of the Aristotelian verisimilar and the Platonic Idea under the metaphor of the golden world, a metaphor which had Christian implications to the humanists. Sidney uses a Fracastorian psychology of the sort analyzed by Hathaway, pp. 316–328, to provide a natural explanation for the poet's perception of this golden world. Hathaway, in his forthcoming "Sidney and the

Golden World," outlines the psychological machinery by which
Sidney's "right" poet uses sensory images (which produced phantasmata according to most commentators) to reflect, by a natural
process, the Platonic Ideas implied by his "golden world." Critics
such as Tomitano, Vieri, and Mazzoni had argued that the will,
directed to virtue, leads the imagination to present images of
Aristotelian universals. The passive intellect and the imagination,
which provide and combine images, are influenced by the will. The
imagination, under the influence of the will, clothes universals in
concrete images, rather than presenting deceptive phantasms.
Sidney implies this process to explain the natural operation of the
mind which allows the poet to imitate the Ideas. Mark Roberts,
"The Pill and the Cherries; Sidney and the Neo-Classical
Tradition," *Essays in Criticism*, XVI (1966), pp. 22–31, and J. P.
MacIntyre, "Sidney's Golden World," *Comparative Literature*, XIV
(1962), pp. 356–365, argue that Sidney conceives of the poet as
imitating the Ideas, and that the techniques of imitation which he
implies are Aristotelian. Sidney subordinates the Aristotelian and
Platonist elements in his theory to a Christian and humanist
vision, however. The Golden World was a common figure. It
symbolized either prelapsarian Paradise or the new reign of Christ,
or both, to many of Sidney's readers (J. E. Hankins, *Shakespeare's
Derived Imagery* [Lawrence, Kan.: University of Kansas Press, 1953],
pp. 274–280). *Loci classici* for the image are Ovid, *Metamorphoses*, I,
89–112, and Virgil, *Eclogues*, IV, 5–7, and commentaries on these
passages. Such commentators as Vives, Landino, and Ascensius
associate the golden world with prelapsarian Eden. The association
probably derives from Augustine (Frank Kermode, *English Pastoral
Poetry* [New York: Barnes & Noble, 1953], p. 27). Sidney's post-
humous collaborator, Arthur Golding, makes the identification
explicit: "Moreover, by the golden age, what other thing is meant/
Than Adam's time in Paradise" (Golding, trans., *Metamorphosis*
[1593], by Ovid, fols. A6^v–A7^r.] Even Sidney's daring comparison
of the poet as creator with God he could have found implied in
Scaliger, *Poetices*, I, i.

(10:2) The Epic heroes Sidney lists here had all exemplified moral
virtues according to their commentators, both openly on the level

of *historia*, and allegorically on the level of *fabula*. Sidney implies the straightforward humanist tradition of commentary which, for example, makes Virgil's Aeneas an exemplar of all the moral virtues, and was commonplace in such commentators as Landino, Vives, and Scaliger (*Poetices*, III, iv, xi). Some of the more mystical Neo-Platonist allegorists drew not only moral, but astrological and numerological truths from epic poetry. Alastair Fowler, *Spenser and the Numbers of Time* (London: Routledge & Kegan Paul, 1964), pp. 63–121, attributes such hermetic allegorizing to Sidney's friend, Spenser.

(10:12) Sidney here implies a natural process which will allow the reader who experiences the poet's imitation of the Ideas of the virtues to embody those virtues in himself. His distinction between delivery directed to the imagination alone and substantial working suggests a theory of psychology rather like that of Gianfrancesco Pico. Pico distinguishes between the intellect, which apprehends truth and is the eye of the soul, and the imagination, which delivers images to the mind from the senses. Such images or phantasms can be used by good angels (G. F. Pico della Mirandola, *On the Imagination*, ed. H. Caplan [New Haven: Yale University Press, 1930], pp. 55–56) to inspire true prophecy and influence the will. Faith can elevate these phantasms to inspire true religion (pp. 89–96). Sidney suggests that the natural faculty of image-making moves the will toward good by a natural process, given the experience of the Ideas of virtue embodied in poetry's speaking picture. Hathaway, *Age of Criticism*, p. 327, argues that Sidney's theory of the imagination bears a closer relationship to the theories of the generation of Fracastoro than to the theories of his contemporaries. Varchi, like Sidney, uses the illustration of castles in the air to identify the fantasy (Hathaway, p. 339). Sidney suggests a natural mechanism by which the images of the Ideas can pass through the sensorium to the intellect and the will. He thus obviates the necessity of some supernatural mechanism, such as the poet's frenzy.

(10:22) Sidney here seems to adapt Anselm's argument to the service of poetry. The poet does not imitate God but rather a prelapsarian nature filled with Ideas of virtue; and his perception is an argument for its existence, and thus for Adam's fall. Spenser's "Garden of Adonis," *Faery Queen*, III, vi, combines the Ideas and primal innocence also. According to Neo-Platonist commentators, God created the universe according to a pattern in his mind (Serranus, *Platonis Opera*, II, 4–5). Guarini compares the poet and God as creators, embodying Ideas in their works (Hathaway, *Age of Criticism*, p. 54). Sidney's argument implies that, as God created Adam in a paradise inhabited with Ideas of virtue, so the poet creates an experience of these Ideas for his reader, and helps the reader embody these Ideas in his own life. Man's natural "erected wit" can influence his "infected will" through the imaginative experience of the Ideas. Sidney drew his "infected will" and "erected wit" from Calvin, *Institutes of the Christian Religion*, II, ii, 12–13 (Shepherd, *Apology*, p. 159). The regenerative power which Sidney here attributes to poetry is similar to the power which commentators on the Bible had attributed to the poetry of the Bible, the Psalms in particular (Tremellius, *Bibliorum*, Part III, pp. 3–5; Pierre Pidoux, *Le Psautier Huguenot* [Basle: 1962], I, 17, 21, 22, 142; II, 9; A. Golding, trans., "Preface," *The Psalmes of David with John Calvin's Commentary* (1571), fol. *iiii^v; Scaliger, *Poetices*, III, cxii).

(11:6) Sidney combines elements from all critical traditions in a single definition. "Imitation" comes ultimately from Aristotle (*Poetics*, I, 1447a) and his commentators; "teach" and "delight" from Horace (*Art of Poetry*, l. 333) and rhetorically inclined commentators on him; Neo-Platonists and rhetoricians had emphasized the metaphor "speaking picture," although it was common to all traditions (Jean H. Hagstrum, *The Sister Arts* [Chicago: University of Chicago Press, 1958], pp. 57–73; Hathaway, *Age of Criticism*, pp. 13–16; Weinberg, *Literary Criticism*, pp. 112, 265, 299). Sidney's immediate source for his eclectic definition might have been Scaliger (*Poetices* I, i), but such eclectic definitions are common in Renaissance theory. Sidney leaves out of this definition the Ciceronian emphasis on "moving" or "persuading" to action, an emphasis central to his theory.

(11:7) Sidney's threefold division of poetry probably comes from

Scaliger, I, i–ii (J. E. Spingarn, *Literary Criticism in the Renaissance*, 2nd ed. [New York: Harcourt, 1963], p. 171), but the division is commonplace in Renaissance literary theory (Weinberg, *Literary Criticism*, pp. 115, 320, 335–336; Serranus, *Platonis Opera*, I, 529). He could have found his Biblical illustrations in Tremellius, *Bibliorum*, Part III, pp. 3–5.

(12:4) Sidney alludes to an argument which continued throughout the Middle Ages and the Renaissance over whether such authors as Lucan and Lucretius, who put explicit discursive statements of fact and philosophy into verse, were poets. Hathaway, *Age of Criticism*, pp. 65–80, gives a thorough account of the argument in the Renaissance. Sidney defines poetry as a "profitable fiction," not as verse, and disagrees with Scaliger, who makes verse the earmark of poetry. Sidney is presumably unwilling to deny that Lucan and Lucretius are poets since they embody a profitable moral lesson, and to that extent, fulfil the function of the poet.

(12:12) The use to which Sidney here puts outward beauty recalls a standard Medieval and Renaissance doctrine of beauty's proper effect. Beauty, used properly, develops images which lead the will and the imagination from the physical to the spiritual virtues, and finally to God. Beauty abused entices the lover, for example, to desire the creature, not the Creator seen through the creature, and thus leads to idolatry, as in the case of Juliet (*Romeo & Juliet*, II.ii.112–115). For a full discussion of this theory of the use of beauty, see D. W. Robertson, *A Preface to Chaucer* (Princeton: Princeton University Press, 1962), pp. 65–113.

(13:10) Sidney's emphasis on "feigning" and the word itself might easily have come from the Pléiade theories discussed by Grahame Castor, *Pléiade Poetics* (Cambridge: Cambridge University Press, 1964), pp. 119 ff.

(13:25) Sidney's "clay lodgings" give a Platonist coloring (*Phaedo*, 82c–83) to a critical commonplace. Scaliger, *Poetices*, VII, ii, remarks that poetry draws men's souls to an Aristotelian beatitude. The elevating effects of poetry and learning are commonly noted (Weinberg, *Literary Criticism*, pp. 8, 282, 303, 429).

(14:5) The astronomer who fell into the ditch was Thales (Plato,

Theatetus, 174a), but the illustration had become commonplace (Shepherd, *Apology*, p. 167).

(16:35) Marguerite Hearsey, "The Defence of Poesie and Amyot's Preface in North's Plutarch," *Studies in Philology*, **XXX** (1933), pp. 535–550, points out relations between Amyot's theory of history and Sidney's argument.

(17:8) The immediate source for this section of the argument is probably Minturno (Smith, *Critical Essays*, I, 389). Sidney adds to Minturno's argument the rhetorical emphasis (Weinberg, *Literary Criticism*, pp. 81, 129) on poetry's power to move. His end, the possession of the sight of the soul, is Neo-Platonist (Weinberg, pp. 264–265).

(17:22) This passage is ambiguous. If Sidney equates the imaginative and judging powers, he is in the Neo-Platonist tradition of psychology (Hathaway, *Age of Criticism*, pp. 342 ff.), but if he separates them, in the Aristotelian (Hathway, pp. 329 ff.).

(17:28) K. O. Myrick, *Sir Philip Sidney as a Literary Craftsman*, 2nd ed. (Lincoln: University of Nebraska Press, 1965), pp. 100–105, identifies Minturno as Sidney's source for this illustration. Sophocles does not bring cattle on to the stage, but Minturno leaves the staging ambiguous and can be read to mean that Ajax does in fact appear on stage whipping cattle.

(18:7) Sidney's list is one of many in Renaissance criticism. Such lists of exemplary characters often developed in connection with Horatian discussions of decorum (Hathaway, *Age of Criticism*, pp. 135–136, 155–156; Weinberg, *Literary Criticism*, pp. 414 ff.). They were also common in medieval discussions of exemplary history.

(18:35) Sidney's tactic of defending poetry by comparing it to New Testament parable is common throughout the Renaissance and Middle Ages. Sidney could have found this defense in Boccaccio (*Geneology*, **XIV**, 9) but it is so common that it is impossible to point to a specific source. (For medieval discussions of the parables and their allegorization, see J. Pepin, *Mythe et Allegorie* [Paris: Montaigne, 1958], pp. 252–259; Robertson, *Preface*, pp. 286 ff.) Sidney argues that "right poetry" and the parables implant virtue through the technique of allegory. Allegory operated to achieve virtue both by praising virtue, and thus arousing a desire to emulate it (O. B. Hardison, *The Enduring Monument* [Chapel Hill: University of North Carolina Press, 1962], pp. 24–42), and by implanting Platonic Ideas in the mind (Rosamund Tuve, *Allegorical Imagery* [Princeton: Princeton University Press, 1966], pp. 28–29, 122 n.).

(19:5) The poet, as popular philospher, not only convinces, but moves. Smith (*Critical Essays*, I, 389) traces Sidney's phrase to Minturno. The idea behind the phrase is common in the Middle Ages and Renaissance.

(19:22) Aristotle, *Poetics*, IX, 1451b. Aristotle emphasizes the poet's obligation to deal with the universal; his discussion became one of the central texts of Renaissance criticism (Hathaway, *Age of Criticism*, pp. 129–200 discusses its influence).

(19:34) Neither the "feigned" Cyrus of Xenophon (*Cyropaedia*) nor the "true" Cyrus of Justin (*Histories*, I, iv–viii) is historically accurate. Xenophon deliberately heightens his narration to make Cyrus an exemplary epic hero, worthy of memory and emulation; Renaissance critics and commentators identified this exemplary use of heightened history as similar to the poets' treatments of Ulysses and Aeneas. Hardison, *Enduring Monument*, pp. 72–77, discusses Cyrus in the Renaissance.

(22:14) Sidney here phrases a commonplace theory of "poetic justice" derived from demonstrative rhetoric (Hathaway, *Age of Criticism*, p. 147) and uses it to attack the historians' moral presumptions, as Agrippa had attacked all secular learning (A. C. Hamilton, "Sidney and Agrippa," *Review of English Studies*, VII [1956], pp. 151–157). Sidney argues that only the poet can give efficacious exemplary proofs. He chooses tyrants who died in their beds, and who were patrons of the arts and learning, to point up the problem and dilemma that an account of their tyranny and learning poses the historian.

(23:21) *Ethics*, I, iii, 1095a. Sidney combines a rhetorical emphasis on persuasion and moving (Shepherd, *Apology*, p. 181; Weinberg, *Literary Criticism*, pp. 81, 129, 134) with his Aristotelian definition.

(24:23) Honey around the rim of a medicine cup (Lucretius, *De rerum natura*, I, 936–950; IV, 11–25) was a commonplace illustration of the use of a charming style, or a charming fable, to convey a medicinable moral point (A. H. Gilbert, *Literary Criticism, Plato to Dryden* [Detroit: Wayne State University Press, 1962], p. 523). Tremellius and Junius use the illustration (*Bibliorum*, Part III, p. 4).

(24:30) Gilbert, *Plato to Dryden*, p. 420, takes "barely" to mean Latin *nudus* and to recall the critical theory which derives poetry's power from its seductive ornamentation. (Hathaway, *Age of Criticism*, pp. 192–195, 71, 77; Weinberg, *Literary Criticism*, pp. 15, 95, 127, discuss this theory). One of Sidney's authorities, Fracastoro, made this ornamentation the distinguishing characteristic of poetry (Girolamo Fracastoro, *Naugerius*, trans. R. Kelso, University of Illinois Studies in Language and Literature, vol. IX [1924], pp. 63–66). Sidney argues that plot, not ornamentation, distinguishes poetry, and does not develop the *res-verba* dichotomy characteristic of the theory which would be implied by *nudus*.

(26:11) This fable was a common rhetorician's example (Shepherd, *Apology*, p. 184; David G. Hale, "Intestine Sedition: The Fable of the Belly," *Comparative Literature Studies*, V [1968], pp. 377–388). Quintilian (*Institutes*, V, xi, 19) couples it with the fables of Aesop as an illustration of the rhetorician's power to sway his audience. A. Thaler, *Shakespeare and Sir Philip Sidney* (Cambridge, Mass.: Harvard University Press, 1947), pp. 6–7, argues that Shakespeare used Sidney's version of the story as the basis for part of *Coriolanus*. Both Sidney and Shakespeare could have found it in schoolboy rhetorical handbooks, including Aphthonius' *Progymnasmata* (R. Rainolde, *Foundacion of Rhetorike* [1563], [New York: Scholars' Reprints, 1945] fol. B2^v).

(26:20) Sidney might have found this commonplace example, from 2 Samuel 1, in Théodore de Bèze, "Praefatio poetica in psalmum davidiis," *Poemata* (Paris, 1567), p. 61. Sidney knew and used the Protestant version of the Psalms by Bèze and Marot in his own translation of the Psalms (J. C. Rathmell, ed., *The Psalms of Sir Philip Sidney* [New York: New York University Press, 1963], pp. xxvi–xxvii).

(27:7) Sidney alludes only briefly to a widespread critical disagreement over the mingling of the genres, specifically in tragicomedy, which became intense among critics (Weinberg, *Literary Criticism* pp. 631, 659–662, 682–684, 1074–1090; Marvin T. Herrick, *Tragicomedy* [Urbana: University of Illinois Press, 1955], pp. 135–142). By dismissing the formal discussion so quickly, Sidney emphasizes his interest in the moral function of poetry.

(27:9) Although lists of the genres are commonplace in Renaissance criticism, Sidney's list seems to have come from Scaliger. Scaliger discusses the elegiac, or what we should call the lyric, poem in *Poetices*, I, i; II, xl; III, cxxv.

(28:10) Sidney distinguishes between the Iamb and Satire on the basis that the Iamb attacks persons, the Satire vices. The Iamb retained its place in Renaissance critical thought in part because Horace (*Epistles*, I, xix, 23–35; *Art of Poetry*, l. 79) alludes to Archilocus and Lycambes, the Iambic poets, whose personal attacks drove their victims to suicide. Scaliger, *Poetices*, I, vii, xii; VI, vii, mentions the distinction between Juvenalian invective (which some critics assigned to the Iamb and Old Comedy) and Horatian irony (which they thought the proper technique in Satire).

(28:13) The Puritan and London city government attack on the stage as a school of abuse is discussed by W. A. Ringler Jr., *Stephen Gosson* (Princeton: Princeton University Press, 1942), p. 110 ff. et passim; Smith, *Critical Essays*, I, xiv–xxi, 61–62.

(28:17) Sidney's definition comes ultimately from Cicero, *De oratore*, II, xiv, 58–59; it is common in the critics who emphasize moral types, persuasion, and social stereotypes in comedy (Hathaway, *Age of Criticism*, pp. 113, 135, 173, 245–246).

(28:26) Scaliger is probably Sidney's source here, since he uses Scaliger's "signifying badge" (Shepherd, *Apology*, p. 189); however Lodge also uses these stock illustrations (Smith, *Critical Essays*, I, 65).

(29:6) Although Sidney bases his discussion of tragedy upon Aristotle (*Poetics*, XIII, 1453a) and Aristotelian commentators and critics such as Robortellus and Scaliger, the ulcer image is drawn from Horace and his commentators, not Aristotle (D. W. Robertson, "Sidney's Ulcer Image," *MLN*, LVI [1941], pp. 56–61).

(29:9) Sidney probably draws his emphasis on admiration and commiseration from Minturno (Smith, *Critical Essays*, I, 392). For a discussion of these terms and their history, see Gilbert, *Plato to Dryden*, pp. 459–461; J. V. Cunningham, *Woe or Wonder* (Denver: University of Denver Press, 1951); Marvin T. Herrick, "Some Neglected Sources of Admiratio," *MLN*, LXII (1947), 222–226. The tradition which lies behind Sidney's terms is complicated. He substitutes them as equivalents for Aristotle's pity and terror. Instead of terror, Sidney wishes to imply awe and to link the affect aroused by tragedy with the divine admiration aroused by other exalted forms of poetry. This awe has a morally impelling, rather than a purely purgative effect.

(29:23) Sidney's lyric is what we should call the ode. He follows Scaliger, *Poetices*, I, xliv.

(30:22) Sidney here merges traditions. Rhetorical and Horatian commentators emphasized poetry's use of proofs by example (Hathaway, *Age of Criticism*, pp. 147, 323). Aristotle and commentators on him emphasized magnanimity as the characteristic heroic virtue, and distinguished it from the more medieval "magnificence" admired by Spenser (Tuve, *Allegorical Imagery*, pp. 57–83). The Epic hero as a perfect example is common in such commentators on Virgil as Landino, Vives, and Fulgentius (Hardison, *Enduring Monument*, pp. 77–80).

(30:35) This opinion of the Epic's primacy is so common that we can only say that it did not come from Castelvetro, who believes tragedy to be the most exalted form of poetry.

(32:27) The paradoxical *encomia* which Sidney has in mind here reflected school-exercises in epideictic rhetoric. Aristotle (*Rhetoric*, I, ix, 1366a) recommends such exercises. They became popular as a literary as well as a schoolroom form in the sixteenth century (H. H. Miller, "The Paradoxical Encomium with special Reference to its Vogue in England, 1600–1800," *Modern Philology*, LII [1956], 145–178).

(33:2) Cornelius Henry Agrippa of Nettesheim (1486?–1535) attacked reason to exalt faith in his *The Vanity and Incertitude of the Sciences and Arts*, trans. J. Sanford (1575), fol. A4ʳ. Agrippa is, like

Erasmus in *The Praise of Folly* and Nicholas of Cusa, in the tradition of *docta ignorantia* and attacks wordly learning and wisdom as obstacles in the path to true wisdom through humility, grace, and faith (Rosalie Colie, *Paradoxica Epidemica* [Princeton: Princeton University Press, 1966], p. 458; Richard H. Popkin, *The History of Skepticism from Erasmus to Descartes* [Assen: Van Gorcum, 1964], pp. 22–25; Walter Kaiser, *Praisers of Folly* [Cambridge, Mass.: Harvard University Press, 1963], passim). Sidney means two things by saying that Erasmus and Agrippa had "another foundation than the superficial part would promise." Erasmus and Agrippa write ironically: Erasmus praises folly to blame it, and Agrippa uses the techniques of secular learning to undermine its pretensions. Erasmus uses a *persona* who is a fool, and Agrippa uses a learned fool's technique to destroy his foolish belief in unGraced learning. Both display men who have no real foundation in faith. The authors, as ironists, also have another foundation; St. Paul's "other foundation." Paul says (I Corinthians, 3:11) "For other foundation can no man lay than that which is laid, which is Christ Jesus." Sidney casts his dispraisers of poetry in the same role as Erasmus's praiser of folly or Agrippa's opponent, the defender of worldly wisdom, who, by the grotesquery of their nature, confirm what they seek to destroy and destroy what they seek to confirm. Sidney drew some of his argumentative techniques from Agrippa (A. C. Hamilton, *The Structure of Allegory in the Faerie Queene* [Oxford: Clarendon, 1961], pp. 19–23).

(33:17) Scaliger, *Poetices*, I, ii.

(33:26) Sidney's emphasis on the soul-ravishing power of music is Neo-Platonist; his emphasis on the regenerative power of the Psalms is Protestant. Aristotelian and rhetorically derived commentaries associated music with purgation (Hathaway, *Age of Criticism*, pp. 51, 55, 57, 331). Neo-Platonist commentaries argued that music cured diseases of mind and body (Hathaway, pp. 208–210). Protestants attributed to the Psalms the power of moving the soul to love God and virtue (Pidoux, *Psautier*, pp. 17, 22, 142; Theodore de Bèze, ed., *The Psalmes of David* [1580], p. Aa2ᵛ; Yates, *Academies*, pp. 36 ff.; Tremellius, *Bibliorum*, Part III, pp. 3–5). Sidney transfers this power to music and poetry. He suggests, like Serranus (*Platonis*

Opera, II, 401) that music implants reason in the soul. Platonist critics considered poetry to be a more efficacious music (Yates, *Academies*, p. 40; P. O. Kristeller, *The Philosophy of Marsilio Ficino* [New York: Columbia University Press, 1943], p. 308).

(34:4) Memory was one of the major divisions of study in the rhetorical curriculum. The mnemonic system which the arts of memory taught depended upon associating the material to be remembered with locations memorized in a walk through a house or room, from which *topoi*, or places, we get "topic." The tour through the house clued the orator to the order of the material he organized and mentally placed in various locations (Frances Yates, *The Art of Memory* [Chicago: University of Chicago Press, 1966]; W. S. Howell, *Logic and Rhetoric in England, 1500–1700* [Princeton: Princeton University Press, 1956], pp. 85–89, 96–98).

(35:10) The charge was commonplace (Shepherd, *Apology*, p. 199). Sidney's argument in defense may have come from Minturno (Shepherd, p. 200). It probably derives through Augustine ("Lying," IV, 4; V, 9; XI, 18 and "Against Lying," X, 24; XIII, 28) and Boccaccio (*Geneology*, XIV, 13). Sidney's argument here recalls his "other foundation" in Erasmus and Agrippa. Sidney attributes affirmation to all the other branches of learning but poetry and implies that imperfect worldly knowledge makes lying inevitable when affirmation is based on it. His argument resembles the arguments of those who exalted faith at the expense of secular wisdom, using sceptic's techniques (Louis Bredvold, *The Intellectual Milieu of John Dryden* [Ann Arbor: University of Michigan Press, 1966], pp. 19–29; Popkin, *Skepticism*, pp. 17–37, discuss the skeptical background of such fideism in the sixteenth century).

(35:25) Sidney takes his image from necromancy. Shakespeare uses the image in *Romeo and Juliet*, II.i.23–24. The image, dealing as it does with black magic, suggests the difference between icastic and fantastic imitation.

(37:7) Sidney's use of the terms "icastic" and "fantastic" reflects a dispute that was developing in Italian critical theory. It is based on Plato (*Sophist*, 235D–236E). Plato defines icastic imitation as a *trompe d'oeil* imitation of physical fact, while fantastic imitation imitates fictions. Sidney's use of the terms reflects the medieval theory that certain sorts of imitation, properly apprehended, plant Ideas of morality in the soul, while fantastic imitation—imitation which fills the sensorium with phantasmata of matter—uses beauty to seduce the soul from virtue (Robertson, *Preface*, pp. 65–80). Tasso and Mazzoni argued about the nature of icastic and fantastic imitation. Sidney agrees with Tasso in making icastic imitation an embodiment of the Ideas of virtue and the good (Hathaway, *Age of Criticism*, pp. 14–16, 120–125, 390–396; Weinberg, *Literary Criticism*, pp. 636–646, 877–883). Cicero, *Orator*, II, 9–11, is a *locus classicus*.

(37:13) Two of these topics were embodied in widely admired Protestant "divine" poetry: Théodore de Bèze, *Abram Sacrifiant* (1550), trans. A. Golding (1577), and Guillaume de Salluste Du Bartas, *La Judit* (1574).

(39:27) Exemplary stories about Scipio were commonplace (Richard Wills, *De re poetica*, ed. A. D. S. Fowler [Oxford: Oxford University Press, 1958], p. 80; Ringler, *Oratio*, p. 86). The figure of Scipio as a heroic figure and an encourager of poetry owes much of its currency to Macrobius's commentary on the *Dream of Scipio*. His immediate fame in the Renaissance was expanded by Petrarch's enthusiasm (Bernardo, *Petrarch*, pp. 9, 111–126).

(45:23) The theory that poetry was a divine gift accompanied by a privileged madness was a Neo-Platonist and humanist commonplace (Hathaway, *Age of Criticism*, pp. 303–390; 431–437; Weinberg, *Literary Criticism*, pp. 250–438) deriving ultimately from Plato's *Ion*. Protestant humanists with whom Sidney sympathized, such as Du Bartas and Buchanan, wished to write Christian "divine" poetry, inspired by the divine frenzy imparted by the Christian muse, Urania. Sidney, in spite of his sympathy for their program, is careful to deny the extraordinary madness of the right poet. He does not wish to replace secular with "divine" poetry, as did many Protestants (Lily B. Campbell, *Divine Poetry and Drama in Sixteenth Century England* [Berkeley: University of California Press, 1959], pp. 5–6). On the other hand, Sidney does not go as far as Castelvetro, who rejected the divine frenzy as a fraud practiced by poets on a naive public.

(46:3) Sidney identifies his Digression as a discussion of rhetorical. and pedagogical methods of teaching and learning to write poetry. The "art" he refers to is the codified body of rules and procedures which one might use in a classroom; "imitation" means the imitation of models in accordance with the methodical analysis found in the art (Howell, *Logic*, pp. 138–145) as was the practice in the formulary rhetorics of the period. Sidney proposes the pedagogic imitation of models, as a freshman composition instructor might use model essays. Sidney here uses imitation as the Pléiade, as well as Italian critics, tended to use it. The Pléiade poets, working from the rhetorical tradition which preceded them in France, tended to define imitation as the imitation of a model poem (Castor, *Pléiade*, pp. 73 ff.), as well as the imitation of the Ideas or Nature. It is this concept of imitation of models which developed into the full-blown neo-classical imitation of the ancients (Hathaway, *Age of Criticism*, pp. 437–459). Some members of the Pléiade proposed a thorough-going programmatic imitation of classical poets as part of a project to re-create classical literature in the French language. Ronsard's *Abrege de l'Art Poetique*, Du Bellay's *Deffence et illustration de l'Langue Francoys*, and Sebillet's *Art Poetique Francoys*, are almost entirely devoted to achieving this kind of neoclassical imitation.

(46:6) The use of exercise to confirm knowledge is a pedagogical commonplace. Sidney may, however, have had in mind the Ramistic theory that exercise is heuristic (W. J. Ong, *Ramus* [Cambridge, Mass.: Harvard University Press, 1958], pp. 263–265).

(46:23) Sidney emphasizes his rhetorical and pedagogical intent. He uses the rhetorician's *res-verba* dichotomy, an analytic tool he avoided earlier. He indicates that Spenser organized clearly (*res*) but that his diction is antiquated (*verba*).

(46:31) Gabriel Harvey recognized Sidney's rhetorical method. He remarked that Sidney is here saying that invention must rule elocution (Smith, *Critical Essays*, I, 360). For Sidney's test of good poetry, its capacity to bear reduction from verse to prose, see Plato, *Republic*, X, 601D.

(47:9) Sidney here uses two of the three unities of neoclassical theory, the unities of time and place. Following Castelvetro and

Scaliger (Smith, *Critical Essays*, I, 398–399) he develops common-sense arguments for trying to keep the action limited to one day and one scene in order to achieve persuasive verisimilitude.

(48:3) Sidney's discussion of Terence is a conflation of Scaliger and Castelvetro (Shepherd, *Apology*, p. 221; Smith, *Critical Essays*, I, 399–400). Sidney confuses Terence's *Eunuch* with his *Heautontimorumenon;* the former takes place in one day, the latter on an evening and the following morning. Renaissance critics, perhaps overly busy, suggested that the play was performed in two parts on successive days. Plautus, in *Captivi*, includes a fifteen-mile journey within the actions supposed in the play.

(48:18) Sidney's discussion of the messenger links him to Castelvetro. Critics, following Horace's commentators, thought the *nuntius* was most useful as a device for avoiding undecorous horrors on the stage. Castelvetro also views the messenger as a technical device which enables the playwright to narrate events necessary to the action, but disruptive of the unities (Gilbert, *Plato to Dryden*, pp. 309, 355).

(49:5) In this discussion of tragicomedy, Sidney summarizes topics that were fully explored in the discussion of Guarini's *Pastor Fido* (Weinberg, *Literary Criticism*, pp. 1074–1090). Sidney is willing to allow the mingling of clowns and kings (with discretion) which is a violation of those rhetorical principles of decorum that were most emphasized in commentaries on Horace. Sidney, by his tolerance, separates himself from the new-budding neoclassicism and its insistence on strict adherence to the rules.

(51:26) These are the faults of the decorated style of rhetorically conceived poetry. Coursing a letter is alliteration. E. K. in his glosses to the *Shepherd's Calendar* condemns "the rakehellye route of our ragged rymers (for so themselves use to hunt the letter)" (Smith, *Critical Essays*, I, 131). "Figures" and "Flowers" are rhetorical terms for verbal devices. "Figure" may refer to acrostics, which had become mildly popular, but more probably refers to organized stylistic devices (Howell, *Logic*, pp. 116–137). Flowers of eloquence were fine decorative verbal effects. Sidney here ridicules the whole formulary rhetoric tradition of poetry, a kind of poetry which he himself wrote upon occasion. On the other hand, so

respected a poet as Mantuan had defended this formulary conception of poetry by arguing that, as God ornaments the world with
blossoms, so the poet uses the flowers of eloquence (*Apologeticon*,
fol. **2^r).

(52:7) Marius Nizolius published *Thesaurus ciceronianus* in 1535. In
it he collected Latin phrases, words and constructions used by
Cicero. The *Thesaurus* was useful to those Renaissance humanists
who prided themselves on imitating Cicero's Latin style, even to the
point of avoiding words, phrases, or sometimes constructions not
found in Cicero's works (H. S. Wilson and C. A. Forbes, *Gabriel
Harvey's Ciceronianus* [Lincoln: University of Nebraska Press, 1945],
pp. 15–30). Sidney admired both Cicero and Demosthenes, but
objected to the Ciceronians' servile habit of making him a model of
verbal correctness rather than of invention and disposition.

(53:27) Sidney disagrees with Ronsard in his commonplace defense
of courtly sprezzatura. Ronsard remarks that to imitate the language
of the courtier is a mistake, since the courtier is presumably better at
fighting than writing (P. Ronsard, *Oeuvres*, ed. G. Cohen [Paris:
Gallimard, 1950], II, 1001).

(54:14) Sidney deals here with topics and arguments which had
interested the Pléiade more than they interested sixteenth-century
Italian critics. The discussions of grammar, the genesis of language,
orthography and pronunciation, of the choice of and imitation of
classical models and genres, were the staples of such critical works of
the Pléiade as Ronsard's *Abrege*, Sebillet's *Art*, Du Bellay's *Deffence
et Illustration*. Sidney's stylistic discussion is reminiscent of the
Pléiade (J. W. H. Atkins, *English Literary Criticism, The Renascence*
[London: Methuen, 1947], p. 133). Sidney's comparison of his
language with Greek and Latin is a commonplace, but the Pléiade
spent more time and emphasis upon this commonplace than did the
Italian critics of the sixteenth century (Du Bellay, *Deffence*, I, ii–iv;
Castor, *Pléiade*, pp. 8–9, 63 ff.). Sidney remarks with pride the
capacity of English to form compound words as a similarity to
Greek. Hall associates Sidney's fondness for compounds with
France (Joseph Hall, "Virigidemiarum," VI, i, 255–256, *Collected
Poems*, ed. A. Davenport [Liverpool: University of Liverpool Press,

1949], pp. 95, 260). Sidney's fondness for compound words could reflect his sympathy for the Protestant humanist and poet, Du Bartas (Guillaume de Salluste du Bartas, *Works*, ed. Holmes et al. [Chapel Hill: University of North Carolina Press, 1935], I, 174–175). Simon Goulart, *The Colonies of Bartas with the Commentaries of S. G.*, trans. W. Lisle (1598), fol. A^v, notices these compound words and their linguistic dignity. The assimilation of one's native language to Latin, Greek, or Hebrew dignity was not, of course, peculiar to the Pléiade; Tyndale, for example, believed that English was closer to Greek than was Latin (Atkins, *Renascence*, p. 97).

(54:26) English critics argued over whether English poetry should be written in rhymed and accented or in quantitative verse (Smith, *Critical Essays*, I, 50, 89, 140, 360). Sidney, following Drant (Sir Philip Sidney, *The Poems*, ed. W. A. Ringler, Jr. [Oxford: Clarendon Press, 1962], pp. 390–393) tried quantitative verse, and he and his friends tried to formulate rules for quantitative verse in English. Sidney here contrasts rhyme and quantity. The discussion concerned the merits of accent (in which one counts stresses) or of quantity (in which one counts, roughly, the time a syllable requires to be pronounced). Sidney's meaning here and the critical discussion were complicated by the fact that "rhyme" could be read to mean "rhythm" or accent. The Pléiade was concerned with the problem of accent and meter at this time (Du Bellay, *Deffence*, II, vii–viii). Sidney's emphasis on the suitability of quantitative verse to music may reflect his interest in the Psalms. Buchanan, Bèze, Marot, and others had attempted to reproduce classical meters in their versions of the Psalms, as Sidney would in his. Accentual meter was characteristic of most Protestant versions of the Psalms (Yates, *Academies*, pp. 90–91), but Protestant English Psalms were distinguished also by their crudity. Sidney discusses metrics more fully in a canceled passage of the *Arcadia*, discovered and printed by Ringler (Sidney, *Poems*, pp. 389–390).

(55:24) Aristotle never says exactly this, although it was a commonplace of criticism. He says something like it in *Metaphysics*, III, iv, 1000a. Sidney probably derives the commonplace from Boccaccio (*Geneology*, xv, 8), who refers to Aristotle for support for the commonplace (Smith *Critical Essays*, I, 402).

(56:2) Sidney characterizes his own opinion of poetry by the obscurity emphasized in medieval and Renaissance Neo-Platonist allegorical interpretations of poetry. Tuve, *Allegorical Imagery*, pp. 41, 122, 219 ff., analyzes the effects of allegorical obscurity. Wills, *De re poetica*, p. 121, phrases the commonplace reflected in Sidney's statement in a more usual and less subtle fashion, making a mechanical equivalence between poetic fiction and the moral or historical truth supposed to be hidden in allegorical poetry. The allegorical obscurity of poetry had commonly figured in defenses of poetry. Ascensius, in his Prologue to Berchorius's *Reductorium Morale*, XV, i, published in 1509 as *De formis figurisque deorum*, quotes Persius on Horace and remarks that moralized fables can be useful even to preachers; he says that the moralization of pagan myth converts the Pantheon into a temple for Saints and gives the stories which we drink in youth a moral use in our age. Hence, he asserts, we should convert Egyptian gold to the use of the Jews, that is, turn these obscure and fabulous tales of the pagans to the use of the Christian Faith (P. Berchorius, *De Formis Figurisque Deorum* [Utrecht, 1960], p. 2). Mantuan defends pagan fables as cloaking scriptural truth (*Apolegeticon*, fol. $**^{r-v}$); Pléiade theorists and Protestant humanists made obscurity a positive virtue, using as sources statements by Jerome, Boccaccio, and others. Ringler, *Oratio*, pp. 74–75, discusses the tradition of this obscurity which might derive proximately from Eusebius, *Oratio Constantini*, 19–21. Such obscurity was acceptable and commendable in philosophers such as Plato, who teach truth through a poetic veil and thus lead men gently and by degrees to dangerous truths (Serranus, *Platonis Opera*, I, xxvi–xxx). Neo-Platonists sometimes verged on treating the revelation cloaked by pagan fables as of equal value with overt Christian revelation. See Jean Seznec, *The Survival of the Pagan Gods* (New York, 1961) pp. 96–101. Du Bartas remarks that the use of allegory ensures that we treat divine mysteries with due reverence, and his translator, Sylvester, elaborates his argument. Golding uses the argument in his Ovid. The effort of solving the allegorical puzzle and piercing the obscurity aids the memory (Golding, *Metamorphosis*, fol. $B2^v$) and scriptural truth hidden under pagan myth lures us to uncover it (fol. $A6^v$). Golding, a compendium of received Protestant opinion, links the obscurity which accompanied allegory to that which accompanied the mysteries of the Psalms (Golding, *Calvin*, fol. *4^v). The Psalms lure us to reveal our own hearts and lift our minds to God, cleared by faith and the meditation provoked by allegorical obscurity.

Bibliography

Guffey, George R. *Elizabethan Bibliographies*, Supplement VII. London: Nether, 1967.

Tannenbaum, Samuel A. *Sir Philip Sidney: A Concise Bibliography*. New York: Tannenbaum, 1941.

A. Primary Editions of the Defense

The Defence of Poesie. London: Ponsonby, 1595. STC 22535.

An Apology for Poetrie. London: Olney, 1595. STC 22534.

The Defence of Poesie. London: Ponsonby, 1595. STC 22534+. This edition consists of the Olney sheets, issued with the Olney title page canceled and the Ponsonby title page added.

"The Defence of Poesie." In *The Countesse of Pembrokes Arcadia . . . with sundry new additions.* London: Ponsonby, 1598. STC 22541.

The Apology for Poetry. Edited by M. R. Mahl, Northridge: San Fernando Valley State College, 1969. An edition of the Norwich MS.

B. Modern Editions of the Defense

An Apology for Poetrie (1595). Edited by E. Arber. London, 1868.

The Defense of Poesy, otherwise known as An Apology for Poetry. Edited by A. S. Cook. Boston, 1890. A modernized conflation of the Ponsonby and Olney texts.

The Defence of Poesie. Edited by E. Shuckburgh. Cambridge, 1891.

"An Apologie for Poetrie." In *Elizabethan Critical Essays*, edited by G. G. Smith, I, 148–207. Oxford: Clarendon Press, 1904.

"The Defence of Poesie." In *The Prose Works of Sir Philip Sidney*, edited by A. Feuillerat, III, 1–49. Cambridge: Cambridge University Press, 1912–1926.

The Defence of Poesie (1595). London: Noel Douglas, 1928. Facsimile of STC 22534+.

"An Apology for Poetry." In *Literary Criticism, Plato to Dryden,* edited by A. H. Gilbert, pp. 404–461. Detroit: Wayne State University Press, 1962.

La Difensa della Poesia. Padua: Silvio Polcardi, 1946.

The Defence of Poesie. Edited by Wolfgang Clemen. Heidelberg: Universität Verlag, 1950.

Un Plaidoyer pour la Poesie. Edited & translated by M. Lebel. Quebec: Laval University Press, 1965.

An Apology for Poetry. Edited by G. Shepherd. London: Nelson, 1965.

A Defence of Poetry. Edited by J. A. Van Dorsten. London: Oxford University Press, 1966. The student of the text should consult the forthcoming edition by Professor William Elwood. Professor Elwood's text will be definitive.

C. Sidney's Poetry

The Poems. Edited by W. A. Ringler Jr. Oxford: Clarendon Press, 1962. The definitive edition.

D. Modern Scholarship

ATKINS, J. W. H. *English Literary Criticism; The Renascence.* London: Methuen, 1947.

BAINE, R. M. "The First Anthologies of English Literary Criticism." *Studies in Bibliography,* III (1951), 262–265.

BLACKBURN, THOMAS H. "Edmund Bolton's *The Cabanet Royal:* A Belated Reply to Sidney's Apology for Poetry." *Studies in the Renaissance,* XIV (1967), pp. 159–171.

BOND, W. H. "The Bibliographical Jungle." *Times Literary Supplement,* September 23, 1949, p. 624.

BUXTON, JOHN. *Sir Philip Sidney and the English Renaissance.* New York: St. Martin's, 1965.

CAMPBELL, LILY, B. *Divine Poetry and Drama in Sixteenth Century England.* Berkeley: University of California Press, 1959.

CASTOR, GRAHAME. *Pléiade Poetics.* Cambridge: Cambridge University Press, 1964.

CHAMBERS, D. "Deffensa de Poesia: A Spanish Version of Sir Philip Sidney's *Defence of Poesie.*" Ph.D. dissertation, University of Kansas. *Dissertation Abstracts,* XVI (1956), 2158.

CLEMENTS, R. J. *Critical Theory and Practice of the Pléiade.* Cambridge, Mass.: Harvard University Press, 1942.

CRAIGIE, J. "Sidney's King James of Scotland." *Times Literary Supplement*, December 20, 1941, p. 648.

DAVIS, W. R. *Sidney's Arcadia.* New Haven: Yale University Press, 1965.

———. *Idea and Act in Elizabethan Fiction.* Princeton: Princeton University Press, 1969.

DOWLIN, C. "Sidney and Other Men's Thought." *Review of English Studies*, XX (1944), 257–271.

———. "Sidney's Two Definitions of Poetry." *Modern Language Quarterly*, III (1942), 573–581.

FOWLER, A. D. S., ED. *De re poetica.* By R. Wills. Oxford: Oxford University Press, 1958.

HALLAM, G. W. "Sidney's Supposed Ramism." In *Renaissance Papers 1963*, pp. 11–21. Durham: Southeastern Renaissance Conference, 1964.

HAMILTON, A. C. "Sidney and Agrippa." *Review of English Studies*, VII (1956), 151–157.

———. "Sidney's Idea of the 'Right Poet'." *Comparative Literature*, IX (1957), 51–59.

HATHAWAY, B. *The Age of Criticism.* Ithaca: Cornell University Press, 1962.

HOGAN, P. "Sidney and Titian: Painting in the *Arcadia* and the *Defence*." *South Central Bulletin*, XXVII, iv (1967), pp. 9–15.

HOWELL, W. S. *Logic and Rhetoric in England, 1500–1700.* Princeton: Princeton University Press, 1956.

KISHLER, T. C. "Aristotle and Sidney on Imitation." *Classical Journal*, LIX (1963), 63–64.

KROUSE, M. "Plato and Sidney's 'Defence of Poesie'." *Comparative Literature*, VI (1954), 138–147.

LEBEL, M. "Sir Philip Sidney et son Plaidoyer pour la Poesie (1595)." *Proceedings and Transactions of the Royal Society of Canada*, ser. IV (1963), pp. 177–186.

LEWIS, C. S. *English Literature in the Sixteenth Century, excluding Drama.* Oxford: Oxford University Press, 1954.

LEVY, F. J. "Sir Philip Sidney and the Idea of History." *Bibliothèque d'Humanisme et Renaissance*, XXVI (1964), 608–617.

McINTYRE, J. P. "Sidney's 'Golden World.'" *Comparative Literature*, XIV (1962), 356–365.

MALLOCH, A. E. "Architectonic Knowledge and Sidney's Apologie." *ELH*, XX (1953), 181–185.

MUIR, K. "Sir Philip Sidney." *British Book News*, CXX (April, 1960).

MYRICK, K. O. *Sir Philip Sidney as a Literary Craftsman*. 2nd ed. Lincoln: University of Nebraska Press, 1965.

NEWELS, K. "Eine Spanische Ubersetzung der 'Defence of Poesie' von Sir Philip Sidney." *Anglia*, LXXII (1954), 463–466.

OSGOOD, C. G., ed. and trans. *Boccaccio on Poetry*. New York: Liberal Arts Press, 1956.

PELLEGRINI, A. "Bruno, Sidney and Spenser." *Studies in Philology*, XL (1943), 128–144.

PHILLIPS, J. E. "Daniel Rogers: A Neo-Latin Link between the Pléiade and Sidney's 'Aereopagus.'" In *Neo-Latin Poetry of the Sixteenth and Seventeenth Centuries*, pp. 5–28. Los Angeles: Clark Memorial Library, 1965.

PONTADERA, C. "Poetica e poesia nel *Apology for Poetry* di Sir Philip Sidney." *Annali di Ca Foscari*, VI (1967), 125–147.

RINGLER, W. A., JR. ed., and W. ALLEN, trans. *Oratio in laudem artis poeticae*. By J. Rainolds. Princeton: Princeton University Press, 1940.

RINGLER, W. A., JR. "Master Drant's Rules." *Philological Quarterly*, XXIX (1950), 70–74.

ROBERTS, M. "The Pill and the Cherries: Sidney and the Neo-Classical Tradition." *Essays in Criticism*, XVI (1966), 22–31.

ROBERTSON, D. W. "Sidney's Metaphor of the Ulcer." *MLN*, LVI (1941), 56–61.

———. *A Preface to Chaucer*. Princeton: Princeton University Press, 1962.

RUDENSTINE, N. *Sidney's Poetic Development*. Cambridge, Mass.: Harvard University Press, 1967.

SAMUEL, I. "The influence of Plato on Sir Phillip Sidney's Defense of Poesy," *Modern Language Quarterly*, I (1940), 383–391.

SASEK, L. *The Literary Temper of the English Puritans*. Baton Rouge: Louisiana State University Press, 1961.

SPINGARN, J. E. *A History of Literary Criticism in the Renaissance*, 2nd ed. New York: Harcourt, 1963.

STROUP, T. "The Speaking Picture Realized: Sidney's 45th Sonnet." *Philological Quarterly*, XXIX (1950), 440–442.

THALER, A. *Shakespeare and Sir Philip Sidney*. Cambridge, Mass.: Harvard University Press, 1947.

THORNE, J. P. "A Ramistical Commentary on Sidney's *An Apologie for Poetrie.*" *Modern Philology*, LIV (1957), 158–164.

TILLYARD, E. M. W. "Sidney's 'Apology.'" *Times Literary Supplement*, June 14, 1941, pp. 287, 290.

TOWNSEND, F. L. "Sidney and Ariosto." *PMLA*, LXI (1946), 97–108.

TUVE, ROSAMUND. *Allegorical Imagery*. Princeton: Princeton University Press, 1966.

WEINBERG, B. *A History of Literary Criticism in the Italian Renaissance*. Chicago: University of Chicago Press, 1961.

YATES, FRANCES. *The Art of Memory*. Chicago: University of Chicago Press, 1966.

———. *The French Academies of the Sixteenth Century*. London: Warburg, 1947.

———. *Giordano Bruno and the Hermetic Tradition*. Chicago: University of Chicago Press, 1964.

ZOLBROD, P. G. "The Poet's Golden World: Classical Bases for Philip Sidney's Literary Theory." Ph.D. dissertation, University of Pittsburgh, 1968. *Dissertation Abstracts*, XXVIII (1968), 5033A.

Index

References to Sidney's text appear in roman type; references to prefatory and explanatory material in italic type.